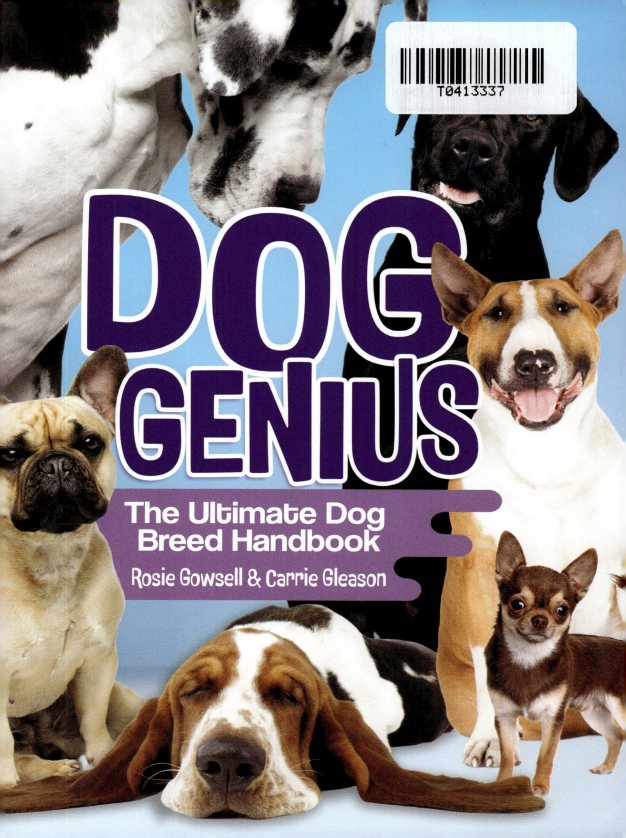

Text copyright © 2026 by North Star Editions. International copyrights reserved in all countries. No part of this book may be reproduced in any form without written permission from the publisher.

First Edition
First Printing, 2026

Editor: Nick Rebman
Designer: Rosie Gowsell

ISBN:
978-1-952455-16-2 (paperback)
978-1-952455-18-6 (pdf)
978-1-952455-17-9 (hosted ebook)

Library of Congress Control Number: 2025931755

Distributed by North Star Editions, Inc.
2297 Waters Drive
Mendota Heights, MN 55120
www.northstareditions.com

Printed in the United States of America

Photo Credits   SS = Shutterstock.com
Cover and p1: (up lt) Eric Isselee/SS, (up rt) Ysbrand Cosijn/SS, (mid rt) Otsphoto/SS, (lo rt) Cynoclub/SS, (lo mid) Artsilense/SS, (lo lt) Svetography/SS; p2: Gelpi/SS; p4 (mid rt) Sue Thatcher/SS, (lo lt) Kristina Chizhmar/SS, (lo rt) Niko Laskus/SS; p5 (up) JR Foto/SS, (lo) Inessa Melikova/SS; p6 (lt) Blue Tick Sugar Images/SS; p7 (up) Alla Sheptiienko/SS, (lo) Veronika Tvrda/SS; p8 (up) Anna Pozzi - Zoophotos/SS, (mid) Belish/SS, (lo) Rosie Gowsell; p9 (up lt) Natallia Yaumenenka/SS, (up rt) LN Bjors/SS, (lo lt) VAKS Stock Agency/SS, (lo rt) Eric Isselee/SS; p10 Annabell Gsoedl/SS; p12 Otsphoto/SS; p13 (up) Aneta Placha/SS, (lo) BigandT.com/SS; p14 Disco Volante/SS; p15 Artsilense/SS; p16 Africa Studio/SS; p18 Radomir Rezny/SS; p20 (up) Dora Zett/SS, (lo) Cade Landers/SS; p21 (up) Lisjatina/SS, (mid) Bennett Walker/SS, (lo) Rebecca Ashworth Earle/SS; p22 Radomir Rezny/SS; p24 Cynoclub/SS; p26 (lt) Tatyana Vyc/SS, (rt) Olga Maksimava/SS; p27 (up rt) Rebecca Ashworth Earle/SS, (mid) Natalia Fedosova/SS, (lo lt) Glenkar/SS; p28 Bear Fotos/SS; p30 Csanad Kiss/SS; p32 (up) Otsphoto/SS, (lo) Vaclav Sonnek/SS; p33 (up) Kachalkina Veronika/SS, (lo) Drazen Boskic Photo/SS; p34 Drazen Boskic Photo/SS; p36 Ivanova N/SS; p38 Svetlanistaya/SS; p40 (up) Peter Turner Photography/SS, (lo) Willee Cole Photography/SS; p41 (up) Mish DP/SS, (mid) Lourdes Photographer/SS, (lo) Taylor Walter/SS; p42 Pardo Y/SS; p44 Eric Isselee/SS; p46 Lenkadan/SS; p48 William Wide/Dreamstime.com; p50 Nikolai Tsvetkov/SS; p52 (up) Rebecca Ashworth Earle/SS, (lo) Alekta/SS; p53 (up) Rosa Frei/SS, (mid) Svetlay/SS, (lo) Wirestock Creators/SS; p54 Liliya Kulianionak/SS; p56 Tatiana Katsai/SS; p57 Eric Isselee/SS; p58 Kuznetsov Alexey/SS; p60 Hanna Dymytrova-Kaihila/SS; p62 Kuznetsov Alexey/SS; p64 Ric Photography/SS; p66 Johann Helason/SS; p68 Liliya Kulianionak/SS; p70 Ricantimages/SS; p72 Eric Isselee/SS; p74 Hugo Felix/SS; p76 Olga Ovcharenko/SS; p78 Happy Monkey/SS; p80 Csanad Kiss/SS; p82 Nataliya Sdobnikova/SS; p84 Cynoclub/SS; p86 (up lt) Orientgold/SS, (up rt) travelarium.ph/SS, (mid lt) Natalia Fesiun/SS, (mid rt) Pardo Y/SS, (lo lt) Mikhail Farina/SS; p87 (up lt) Eudyptula/SS, (up rt) Devor 1/SS, (mid lt) Aneta Zabranska/SS, (mid rt) Eve Photography/SS, (lo) Zanna Pesnina/SS; p88 Debra Anderson/SS; p90 Sue Thatcher/SS; p91 (up) Lourdes Photography/SS; (lo) Francine Parent; p92 Eric Isselee/SS; p94 Natallia Yaumenenka/SS; p96 Marharyta Manukha/SS; p98 Alias Studio Oy/SS; p100 (up) Anna Averianova/SS, (lo) Msgra Fixx/SS; p101 (up) V Karlov/SS, (lo) Rita Kochmarjova/SS; p102 Dmitry Kalinovsky/SS; p104 Dien/SS; p106 Tanya Consual Photography/SS; p108 (lt) Rosie Gowsell; (rt) GoDog Photo/SS; p109 (up) Photobox.ks/SS, (mid) Aneta Jungerova/SS, Sanjagruic/SS; p110 Master 1305/SS; p112 Eric Isselee/SS; p114 Golland/SS; p116 Toloubaev Stanislav/SS; p118 Ermolaev Alexander/SS; p120 Seregraff/SS; p122 Tatiana Gasich/SS; p124 Suti Stock Photo/SS; p126 (up) Mariia Kenig/SS, (lo) Oasisamuel/SS; p127 (up) Kwadrat/SS, (mid) Olga Aniven/SS, (lo) Linas T/SS; p128 Dorottya Mathe/SS; p130 Degtyaryov Andrey/SS; p132 Andy Bir/SS; p134 BigandT.com/SS; p136 (up) Didkovska Ilona/SS, (lo) Dark Side/SS; p137 (up) Lisjatina/SS, (lo) Olga Aniven/SS; p138 Ots Photo/SS; p140 Tanya Consual Photography/SS; p142 Dora Zett/SS; p144 Willee Cole Photography/SS; p146 Eric Isselee/SS; p148-151 Natallia Yaumenenka/SS; p152 Chris UK Photo/SS; p154 Irina Vaneeva/SS; p156 Kuznetsov Alexey/SS; p158 Rita Kochmarjova/SS; p159 Marcelino Pozo Ruiz/SS; p160 (up) Viktoriia Drobotova/SS, (lo) Felipe Cabral/SS; p161 (up) Sue Thatcher/SS, (lo) William F. Cermak/SS; p162 Gleb Semenjuk/SS; p164 Eric Isselee/SS; p166 Kuznetsov Alexey/SS; p168 Streamroller Blues/SS; p170 Eric Isselee/SS; p172 Chase D'animulls/SS; p174 Tanya Consaul Photography/SS; p176 J. Photos/SS; p178 Cynoclub/SS; p180 Andrey Skat/SS; p182 Borina Olga/SS; p184 (up) Lindaze/SS, (mid) Aneta Jungerova/SS, (lo) Anetapics/SS; p185 (up lt and rt) Sue Thatcher/SS, (lo lt) Vera Reva/SS, (lo rt) Lisjatina/SS; p186 (up lt) Jennifer McCallum/SS, (up rt) Evenii And/SS, (lo lt) Andrew0004/SS, (lo rt) Fluechter Photography/SS; p187 (up lt) Adree 1985/SS, (up rt) Chedko/SS, (mid lt) Maria Bell/SS, (mid rt) Jaclyn Vernace/SS, (lo lt) Chris UK Photo/SS, (lo rt) Steve Bruckmann/SS; p188 Mary Dimitropoulou/SS; p189 (up) Robert Hoetink/SS, (lo) Michael Keatley/SS.

Contents

Meet the Breeds 4

SPORTING GROUP p. 10

Retrievers 12
- Labrador Retriever 14
- Golden Retriever 16
- Chesapeake Bay Retriever 18

Spaniels 20
- Brittany 22
- Cocker Spaniel 24

Setters 26
- Irish Setter 28
- English Setter 30

Pointers 32
- German Shorthaired Pointer 34
- Vizsla 36

HOUND GROUP p. 38

Scent Hounds 40
- Beagle 42
- Basset Hound 44
- Bloodhound 46
- Treeing Walker Coonhound 48
- Dachshund 50

Sight Hounds 52
- Greyhound 54
- Rhodesian Ridgeback ... 56
- Irish Wolfhound 58
- Pharaoh Hound 60
- Afghan Hound 62

WORKING GROUP p. 64

- Doberman Pinscher 66
- Rottweiler 68
- Mastiff 70
- Great Dane 72
- Boxer 74
- Cane Corso 76
- Bernese Mountain Dog 78
- Saint Bernard 80
- Siberian Husky 82
- Anatolian Shepherd 84

More Working Dogs 86

TERRIER GROUP p. 88

Short-Legged 90
- Cairn Terrier 92
- Scottish Terrier 94
- West Highland Terrier ... 96
- Russell Terrier 98

Long-Legged 100
- Airedale 102
- Soft-Coated Wheaten Terrier 104
- Rat Terrier 106

Bull-Type 108
- Bull Terrier 110
- Staffordshire Bull Terrier 112

TOY GROUP p. 114

- Yorkshire Terrier 116
- Pug 118
- Chihuahua 120
- Shih Tzu 122
- Pomeranian 124

Mini-Versions 126
- Havanese 128
- Maltese 130
- Papillon 132
- Cavalier King Charles Spaniel 134

More Toy Breeds 136

NON-SPORTING GROUP p. 138

- French Bulldog 140
- Boston Terrier 142
- Bulldog 144
- Bichon Frise 146
- Lhasa Apso 148
- Poodle 150
- Dalmatian 152
- Shiba Inu 154
- Xoloitzcuintli 156
- Chinese Shar-Pei 158

More Non-Sporting Dogs 160

HERDING GROUP p. 162

- German Shepherd 164
- Pembroke Welsh Corgi 166
- Collie 168
- Australian Shepherd 170
- Border Collie 172
- Australian Cattle Dog 174
- Belgian Malinois 176
- Bouvier des Flandres 178
- Old English Sheepdog 180
- Puli 182

More Herders 184

Mixed Breeds 186

Adopting 188

Glossary 190

Index 192

MEET THE BREEDS

The feisty little Chihuahua and the giant gentle Newfoundland look very different from each other and have distinct personality traits, but they are the same species. They're both *Canis lupus familiaris,* more commonly known as dogs. It may be hard to believe by looking at the hundreds of different breeds that exist today, but all dogs come from a common, wolf-like ancestor. So, how did we get from wolf to Chihuahua?

In from the Wild

A breed, such as a Chihuahua or a Newfoundland, is a type of dog that was selectively produced by humans for a specific purpose. Dogs were domesticated at least 15,000 years ago by people in different parts of the world. Domesticated animals, which include cows, horses, cats, and dogs, have been adapted over a long period of time for use by humans. Only animals that have been domesticated have breeds. People began breeding different types of dogs at least 9,500 years ago. The earliest dog breeds were used for work, such as providing protection for homes and livestock, or for hunting and tracking food to eat. Today, there are about 400 recognized dog breeds worldwide and countless other mixed breeds.

Chow Chow

Akita

Tibetan Mastiff

Breed Standards

New dog breeds were created by mating dogs with certain characteristics. For example, border collies were bred for their speed so that they could work over large areas. Corgis, with their little legs, were bred to be short so they could nip at livestock's legs. In the early 1800s, people in England started breeding dogs just for show. Toy dogs, such as the adorable and friendly Cavalier King Charles Spaniel, were bred from sporting dogs to be lovable and lightweight companions. Today, each breed has specific standards that describe the characteristics of the type of dog.

Cavalier King Charles Spaniel

Cardigan Welsh Corgi

American Kennel Club

In countries around the world, kennel clubs have been established to maintain breed standards for purebred dogs. The American Kennel Club, or AKC, is a not-for-profit purebred dog registry. It provides information about breeds, canine health, dog sports, training, and more. As of 2024, the American Kennel Club recognized 200 breeds in its registry. The dog breeds the AKC recognizes depends on how popular that breed is in the United States. Recognized breeds are divided into seven groups based on physical and personality traits. These groups are the sporting, hound, working, terrier, toy, non-sporting, and herding groups.

SPORTING GROUP

Dogs in the sporting group were originally bred as far back as the 1600s to help hunters find, flush out, and retrieve game on land or in water. Many sporting dogs still perform these duties today, but they are also some of the most popular choices for family pets.

HOUND GROUP

Dogs in the hound group use their keen sense of sight or smell to track and hunt prey. Sight hounds spot their prey and chase it down, while scent hounds catch a scent and follow their prey while a human follows. These dogs have a strong prey drive and will often stop at nothing to catch their target.

WORKING GROUP

Working group dogs are some of the oldest breeds in the world. They are powerful and sturdy dogs that were originally bred to help people perform various tasks such as protection and pulling carts.

TERRIER GROUP

Terriers come in many shapes and sizes, but all can be described as determined and feisty. The word *terrier* comes from the Latin word *terra*, which means "earth." Most terriers were bred to burrow into the ground to catch vermin such as rats, badgers, and weasels.

TOY GROUP

Toy dogs are small enough to fit on people's laps and are diverse in appearance. Many toy breeds have been around for centuries to serve as companions. Some are miniature versions of larger breeds. Their small size makes them popular pets for people with limited space.

NON-SPORTING GROUP

Non-sporting dogs don't fit neatly into any of the other six groups. They have varied job descriptions, histories, physical characteristics, and personality traits. Some may have been bred as working dogs in the past, but now they're mainly companion animals.

HERDING GROUP

Some dogs have a natural instinct to herd animals, so these dogs are ideal for moving livestock such as sheep and cattle from one place to another on farms and ranches. Herding dogs are intelligent and high energy, making them easily trainable for this task.

Working Dogs

People still use many dogs for work. On farms, dogs are used for herding and protecting livestock. Hunters use dogs to track and retrieve small game, such as birds and ducks. Dogs are used in police work, search-and-rescue operations, and for security. Dogs are also used to guard people and property. Service dogs are trained to help people with disabilities. Therapy dogs provide affection, comfort, and ease for people with conditions such as anxiety. Different breeds of dogs are suited for specific jobs.

Hunting Dog

Search-and-Rescue Dog

Dog Show Winner

Sport Competitions and Shows

If you like dogs, there's nothing quite as exciting as a dog sport competition. These events showcase the natural athleticism of dogs. At dog sport competitions, dogs participate in a number of different feats. In agility competitions, handlers direct their dogs through an obstacle course made up of hurdles, walkways, and tunnels. In the canine freestyle event, handlers give their dogs a series of commands for jumping, walking backward, weaving through the handler's legs, or performing twists and turns. Flyball is a four-dog relay race down a 51-foot (15.5-m) track. One at a time, dogs run down the course, jump over four hurdles, hit the flyball box with their paws to release a tennis ball, and return with the ball to the start. It takes all four dogs just 24 seconds or less to finish! In tracking or scent events, dogs follow a scent trail or find hidden scents in various environments and containers. Meanwhile, at dog shows, judges evaluate dogs based on breed standards such as size, build, and appearance. Awards are given to dogs in different breed, age, and sex categories. The top dogs from each category then stand a chance of winning Best in Show—the dog show's top dog award!

Flyball

Canine Freestyle

Police Dog

Guide Dog

Dogs as Pets

Choosing which breed to get as a pet is a big decision. Does the person want a dog that needs plenty of exercise, or one that is a little bit on the lazy side? How much time will the person have to make sure the dog gets enough attention? Trainability, or how easy a dog is to train, is also an important quality when deciding on a breed. Some dogs may be stubborn or easily distracted, so they don't learn quickly. Beagles, for example, are so distracted by the scents around them that they may find it hard to focus on learning new tasks. Others, such as the Labrador retriever, are so eager to please their humans that they learn quickly. Knowing what a type of dog was originally bred to do is an excellent way to figure out whether a dog will be a good fit for someone's lifestyle.

SPORTING GROUP

Sometimes referred to as gundogs or bird dogs, breeds in the sporting group are alert, naturally active, and athletic. These dogs were originally bred to work alongside hunters to find and retrieve game. Eager to please, a sporting dog will throw itself into dense brush to flush out fowl or dive into frigid waters to retrieve a downed bird for its human. Most of these highly energetic breeds are resilient to harsh weather and have well-insulated, water-repellent coats. Their floppy ears protect their ear canals by keeping out dirt and debris while they swim or run through fields. Dogs in the sporting group require frequent walks and lots of brisk activity to keep them healthy and happy.

There are four types of sporting dogs:

1. Retrievers
2. Spaniels
3. Setters
4. Pointers

Many of the most popular breeds in North America are members of the sporting group. When not used for hunting, these breeds make great family pets—as long as they get enough exercise! They are friendly, easy to train, and great with children.

- sporting group
- hound group
- working group
- terrier group
- toy group
- non-sporting group
- herding group

Retrievers

Retrievers are a type of gundog that were bred specifically to retrieve game for hunters. They bring back small animals and birds that have been shot, especially waterfowl. So, it comes as no surprise that these dogs are also great swimmers. Their thick, water-repellent coats are resistant to harsh hunting conditions, and their webbed feet help them paddle in the water.

Curly-Coated Retriever
The curly-coated retriever is the oldest member of the retriever group. It is believed to have been crossed with a poodle to get its tight, curly coat. The curls help make its coat waterproof in water and resistant to thorns in underbrush.

Nova Scotia Duck Tolling Retriever

The Nova Scotia duck tolling retriever is the smallest of all the retrievers. The word *tolling* comes from the old English word *tollen*, meaning "to lure," which is what these dogs were originally bred to do. Hunters would play fetch with them along the shoreline, and the movement of the dogs' fluffy tails and red coats would lure ducks to the shore within shooting range. Today, these energetic, loving dogs are still happy to play fetch or hunt for hours on end.

Flat-Coated Retriever

This cheerful and energetic dog looks a lot like his golden retriever cousin, but there are some differences. A flat-coated retriever's sleek, shiny coat comes in black or liver (a reddish-brown color), and it lays flat without the distinctive feathering of the golden retriever. The flat-coated retriever also has a longer head and a larger body. This dog is highly intelligent, affectionate, and easily trainable like the golden retriever, but it is more independent.

Labrador Retriever

Meet the Labrador retriever! Often called Labs, these athletic pooches are one of the most popular members of the sporting group in the United States. Labradors are friendly, high-energy dogs that love to swim. They were originally bred for their ability to retrieve waterfowl for hunters, but their lovable personalities and trainability make them a top choice for family pets, therapy dogs, and a variety of other jobs.

otter tail
The thick, sturdy tail is used like a rudder on a boat to help a Labrador swim.

double coat
Labs are known as water dogs and have double coats. This means they have an inner layer of short, soft fur covered by a longer, tougher outer layer. The double coat acts as a waterproof barrier that keeps the dog warm while it's swimming in cold water.

webbed feet
Labs have skin between their toes to help them swim like ducks. While Labs swim, their toes spread out, and the webbing helps push against the water to propel them forward.

intelligent
Labs are very smart and eager to please their humans, which makes them easy to train. This has made them a top choice as service and guide dogs.

sniffy nose
Labs have an instinct to sniff out a target and retrieve it. That makes Labs ideal for use as search-and-rescue dogs, scent dogs for the military, and arson and bomb detection dogs.

soft mouth
Labrador retrievers are known for having "soft mouths." This means they can hold things in their mouths with a light grip, so they don't cause any damage to what they're holding. A Lab can even hold an egg in its mouth without breaking it!

🐾 Paws for Thought 🐾
Labs come in three colors: chocolate (brown), black, and yellow. One litter of Labradorables can include all three coat colors.

Golden Retriever

The golden retriever is one of the top three most popular dogs in North America. Their natural zest for outdoor play, swimming, and fetching make them the perfect companion for hunters retrieving waterfowl. Goldens are easily trainable, obedient, and eager to please. These days, golden retrievers are still used for hunting, but they can also be found working as search-and-rescue dogs and as guide dogs for the blind.

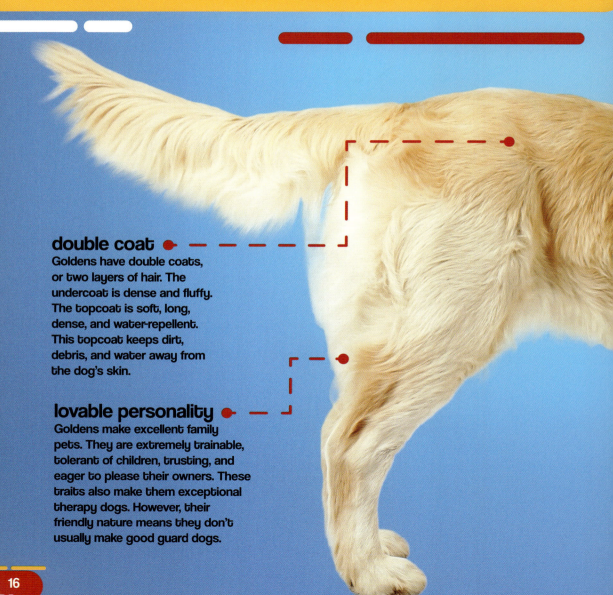

double coat
Goldens have double coats, or two layers of hair. The undercoat is dense and fluffy. The topcoat is soft, long, dense, and water-repellent. This topcoat keeps dirt, debris, and water away from the dog's skin.

lovable personality
Goldens make excellent family pets. They are extremely trainable, tolerant of children, trusting, and eager to please their owners. These traits also make them exceptional therapy dogs. However, their friendly nature means they don't usually make good guard dogs.

born to be famous
Goldens are considered to be one of the five smartest breeds, which makes them easy to train and a popular choice for TV and movies.

three flavors
Golden retrievers come in three colors: cream, yellow, or gold.

super-sniffers
The golden retriever has a keen sense of smell and exceptional tracking abilities. Like the Labrador retriever, the golden retriever also has a lot of energy and an intense drive to find and retrieve objects. This focused energy makes the breed the perfect choice for search-and-rescue jobs.

🐾 Paws for Thought 🐾

Golden retrievers have been known to "adopt" other animals and take care of them, including abandoned kittens, a tiger cub, and even a litter of African painted dog pups!

Chesapeake Bay Retriever

This curly-coated cutie is not only good looking but also a highly athletic and powerful dog. The Chesapeake Bay retriever is named for the area of the mid-Atlantic region of the United States where they were first bred. Originally used to hunt and retrieve waterfowl from the choppy waters of the Chesapeake Bay, these dogs think nothing of splashing into chilly water!

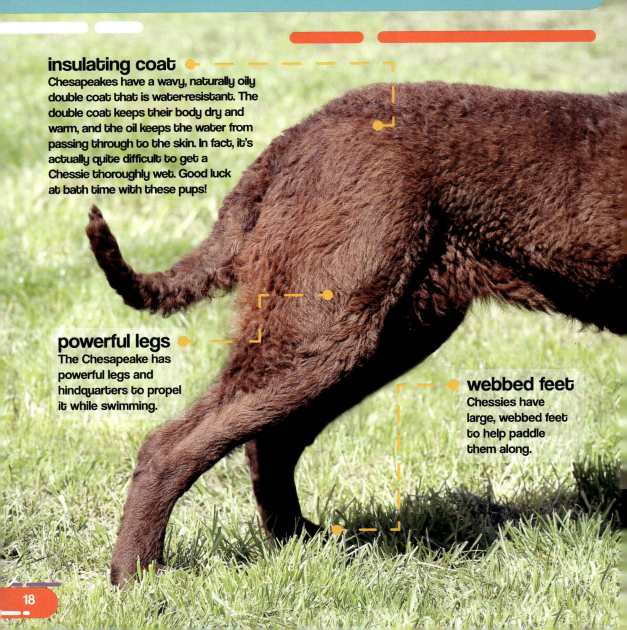

insulating coat
Chesapeakes have a wavy, naturally oily double coat that is water-resistant. The double coat keeps their body dry and warm, and the oil keeps the water from passing through to the skin. In fact, it's actually quite difficult to get a Chessie thoroughly wet. Good luck at bath time with these pups!

powerful legs
The Chesapeake has powerful legs and hindquarters to propel it while swimming.

webbed feet
Chessies have large, webbed feet to help paddle them along.

cool eyes
A Chesapeake's eyes are yellow or amber.

personality
Chessies aren't as outgoing as other retrievers and are often described as having minds of their own.

strong chest
The Chessie has a broad, strong chest that was built to act as a plow to bust through surface ice while swimming in the frigid water of the Chesapeake Bay.

🐾 Paws for Thought 🐾
The Chesapeake Bay retriever is the official state dog of Maryland.

Spaniels

Spaniels are the oldest of the sporting breeds. They are gundogs bred to find and flush out game in the grasslands where certain birds nest. Spaniels can be divided into land spaniels and water spaniels, but some are multitaskers and can hunt on both land and in water. Some spaniels, such as the cocker and clumber spaniel, have shorter legs for wriggling through thickets and brush. Others, including the Brittany and springer spaniel, have longer legs so they can cover more ground.

Clumber Spaniel

This heavy, long, low-to-the-ground spaniel has a massive head that's built to push into thick ground cover to find game. Clumbers are powerful bird dogs with a sweet, easygoing personality. They are eager to please but can be relentless when following a scent.

Boykin Spaniel

The Boykin is a medium-sized water spaniel bred to work in the lakes and swamps of South Carolina. Boykins are strong-willed hunters, excellent swimmers, and sweet pets. Originally known only in South Carolina, the Boykin has become popular around the world. South Carolina was so proud of its dog that lawmakers made it the official state dog and declared September 1 as Boykin Spaniel Day.

Nederlandse Kooikerhondje

Pronounced "Nay-der-lands-say koy-ker-hoon-je," this dog breed's name translates loosely to "decoy dog." They were originally bred in the Netherlands to lure ducks into cages, or "kooi," for the hunter. The dog's plumed white tail and playful movements would attract the ducks into the cages.

American Water Spaniel

The American water spaniel is a medium-sized gundog that comes from the lake area of the upper Midwest in the United States. Its curly coat helps keep it waterproof while swimming and retrieving downed waterfowl in the cold water of the Great Lakes.

English Springer Spaniel

Springer spaniels are eager and reliable gundogs. They find game birds in tall grass and flush or "spring" the birds from their hiding spots and retrieve them. They are tireless and content to hunt on land or in streams all day. When not hunting, these highly trainable dogs are people pleasers, happy to be with their families.

Brittany

The Brittany is one of the most diverse sporting dogs because it is considered an all-purpose worker. It can retrieve ducks and birds both on land and in water. This little spaniel is most prized for its stamina and its ability to flush out birds in hunting fields. The Brittany also shines in competitive dog sports such as agility, flyball, and diving. The Brittany is known for its sweet personality.

coat
The Brittany has a medium-length coat that is flat or slightly wavy. They come in five colors: orange and white, liver and white, black and white, tricolor (black, tan and white), or a "roan" of any of these colors. A roan is one main color mixed with hairs of other colors.

stamina
Brittanys have a lot of energy and require a minimum of an hour of vigorous exercise every day. Without exercise, Britts have been known to develop behavioral problems out of boredom, such as too much barking.

intelligent
Brittanys are easily trainable for many tasks, including hunting, sports, and obedience. They are also very loyal and affectionate and love to be around their humans.

inquisitive sniffer
The Britt's nose is a smelling machine. It is constantly picking up new smells, and this dog will follow that smell right out of sight if you aren't watching!

super sensitive
Brittanys have a gentle nature and are extremely patient dogs, but they don't react well to raised voices. They crave companionship and do not do well with being left alone for long periods of time.

🐾 Paws for Thought 🐾
Young Brittanys have been known to suddenly pee when they get overexcited or feel scared! This is called excitable or submissive urination, and the dog usually grows out of it.

Cocker Spaniel

The cocker spaniel was introduced to the United States from England in the late 1800s. The word *cocker* comes from a game bird called a woodcock, which these dogs were originally used for flushing out. Today, while they're still used as hunting dogs, these affectionate and lovable dogs are popular family pets that are famous for their cheery disposition.

big dogs in small packages
Standing only 14 to 15 inches (35–38 cm) tall, the cocker spaniel is one of the smallest sporting spaniels. But don't be fooled by their size! They are solid, sturdy, and athletic dogs. They are capable of running at considerable speeds and have plenty of endurance.

energetic
Although a popular family pet, a cocker spaniel was built for sport. The cocker spaniel is a playful, active, alert dog that requires a brisk daily walk or a run in a field to keep the mind and body engaged.

coat of many colors
Cocker spaniels come in many colors: red, brown, black, silver, buff (cream-colored), brown, or any combination of these colors with white. They also require regular grooming to keep their silky hair from getting matted.

eager to please
Cocker spaniels are a breed that must have human companionship. They are eager to please their humans and may become sensitive to reprimands. Training them in a firm but kind way will help them become loyal, obedient dogs.

long ears
These super-soft, long ears are just begging to be touched! But they aren't just for show. Like most dogs with long ears, these ears dangle along the ground and collect scents near the nose while the dog is hunting. They also block out sound to help the dog focus on scent.

🐾 Paws for Thought 🐾
Cocker spaniels became popular in the 1950s when the Disney film *Lady and the Tramp* was released. Lady was a cocker spaniel.

Setters

Setters are a type of hunting dog that were bred before guns were used for hunting. The name *setter* comes from how these dogs snuck up on birds and then "set down" on their bellies and stared intently at the birds' location to alert the hunter. The hunter would then throw a net over the entire area, including the dog, to trap the birds. A dog lying on its belly was easier to get out of the net than a dog that was standing up.

Gordon Setter

The Gordon is the largest and strongest of the setters and is instantly recognizable by its black and tan coat. They were bred to withstand bad weather while hunting birds slowly and intently in the rough Scottish landscape. The Gordon also makes a good watchdog. They are extremely loyal and very protective of their families. They have a calmer temperament than other setters, but these dogs are intelligent and can be a bit stubborn. Training and patience is a must!

Irish Red and White Setter

The Irish red and white setter is considered the original Irish setter. The Irish setter and the Irish red and white setter co-existed for a long time and are nearly identical, but the Irish setter was more popular because of its gorgeous red coat. The red and white setter nearly became extinct by the end of the 1800s, but hunters brought it back because its coat was easier to spot in the fields. In the 1980s, Irish red and white setters were introduced to the United States.

Irish Setter

The Irish setter is an outgoing, affectionate, and sensitive dog that is always ready to hunt or play with its human. Originally bred in the 1800s to work alongside trained falcons and hunters with nets, these dogs are efficient and tireless hunting sidekicks in the fields. They're also devoted, active, and playful companions at home.

coat
Although most famous for their long, silky, flowing red hair, Irish setters can also be mahogany or chestnut. Irish setters need brushing at least twice every week to prevent mats.

long legs
Irish setters have long, powerful back legs. This muscular rear-wheel drive helps make Irish setters one of the swiftest of all sporting dogs.

long ears
These long ears, which reach nearly to the end of the Irish setter's nose when its head is down, help to funnel scents directly into its nostrils.

strong nose
Red's strong nose makes it a superb bird dog, able to find and flush out fowl with great skill.

kid at heart
Irish setters are slow to mature and are often described as rambunctious and stubborn until the age of three. They are also very affectionate and are intended to work closely with people.

🐾 Paws for Thought 🐾

Four US presidents have owned Irish setters. Franklin D. Roosevelt had two Irish setters named Jack and Jill. Harry S. Truman named his dog Mike. Richard Nixon's dog, King Timahoe, was named after a small town in Ireland. And Ronald Reagan's Irish setter was called Peggy.

English Setter

Called the gentleman of the dog world because of its gentle, affectionate personality, the English setter is not only an agile hunting partner but also a loving family member that thrives on companionship. The English setter is one of the oldest breeds of setter, with a history dating back 400 years. They developed over the years to become masters at setting and retrieving game birds.

medium build
The English setter is the smallest of the four types of setters. It is considered a medium-sized dog, while the Irish, Gordon, and Irish red and white setters are considered large dogs.

belton beauty
The word *belton* is unique to the English setter. It refers to the speckled coat pattern of this breed. English setters can be orange belton (white and tan, shown here), blue belton (white with black speckles), tricolor (blue with tan on the muzzle, eyes, and legs), liver, or lemon belton.

grooming
Despite its long beautiful coat, a weekly brushing is enough to keep the English setter free of tangles and mats.

upward sniffer
While hunting, you'll find the English setter with its nose in the air. Since it hunts mainly grouse, pheasant, and quail, it tracks these birds through airborne scents.

personality
The English setter is well known for its gentle and loving nature. They crave affection—both giving it and getting it—and form strong bonds with their humans. This makes them an excellent choice for therapy dogs and families with children.

🐾 Paws for Thought 🐾
The English setter is one of the original nine dogs registered with the American Kennel Club in 1878.

Pointers

Pointers are gundogs that, as their name suggests, point! When a pointer picks up a scent, it stands completely still, lifts a front leg, raises its tail, and points its nose in the direction of the game. They also are willing to hunt over any terrain in any weather. These breeds are usually high-energy, athletic, and intelligent dogs. Pointers make loving companions and are extremely loyal to their humans.

Pointer
Imagine being so good at your job that you are named after it! That's the case with the pointer. The pointer has been pointing at game birds and hares for centuries. But pointing isn't all this dog does. This athletic and cheerful dog is also the perfect running companion and is used for search-and-rescue.

Wirehaired Pointing Griffon
This medium-sized gundog is a skilled hunter both on land and in the water. Wirehaired pointing griffons are intelligent, hardworking, and require lots of daily exercise to burn off all the energy they have. The breed is an excellent choice for a family pet. They are calm and laid-back companions while at home, but their gentle temperament may not make them great watchdogs.

Bracco Italiano

The bracco Italiano's name means "Italian pointing dog" in Italian. This is a large-sized pointer from Italy and is one of the oldest pointing breeds, with a history dating back more than 6,000 years. Braccos are playful, loyal, highly intelligent, and stubborn. They also have endless amounts of energy and need a lot of daily exercise to keep them happy.

German Wirehaired Pointer

The German wirehaired pointer is a versatile gundog that is at home in the outdoors. The wiry coat was meant to act as a waterproof suit of armor against thorny brush in the field, foul weather on land, and water while swimming. German wirehaired pointers have endless energy. If not used for hunting, they excel at dog sports or with an active family. They are even-tempered and loyal to their family.

German Shorthaired Pointer

The German shorthaired pointer, or GSP, was bred in Germany in the 1800s to be an all-purpose gundog. The result was an intelligent, gentle breed that can hunt, point, and retrieve on any type of terrain—field, woods, land, or water. This highly active and versatile dog is an excellent family pet, which is why it is still one of the most popular sporting dogs today.

born athlete
The GSP has a muscular body that is great for running, swimming, and even climbing. They have incredible endurance and can walk or hunt for hours.

webbed feet
GSPs have webbed feet to help them paddle through the water, making them excellent swimmers.

beautiful coat
The German shorthaired pointer has a short coat that is a solid liver (reddish-brown) color. It can also be liver and white with a speckled pattern. This speckled pattern is called ticking. Their coats require minimal grooming, but they do shed quite a bit.

intense hunter
The GSP has keen hunting instincts and will stop at nothing to go after its prey. They have been known to scale a fence or a wall while giving chase! Because of this strong prey drive, it's a good idea to keep your GSP on a leash while out for a walk.

endless energy
One walk a day isn't enough for a GSP. In fact, it's nearly impossible to tire one out. If not used as a hunting dog, a GSP will excel at competitive dog sports. They are great family dogs for people who live active lifestyles and enjoy running, cycling, and hiking.

🐾 Paws for Thought 🐾
Even though they are proven duck dogs, German shorthaired pointers will hunt and retrieve a variety of small animals, including raccoons, game birds, and rabbits. They have even been known to help hunt game as large as deer!

Vizsla

The vizsla is an ancient Hungarian hunting dog introduced to North American in the 1950s. Bred for speed, agility, and toughness, this dog is also an extremely devoted companion. In fact, most owners say that the *V* in vizsla stands for Velcro! These dogs form tight bonds with their owners. Vizslas do not like to be left alone and will often follow people from room to room.

running machines
With their lean, athletic bodies and great stamina, vizslas are built for running. They can reach a top speed of 40 miles per hour (64 km/h), making them one of the top 10 fastest dog breeds. This dog is great for people looking for jogging companion . . . if you can keep up!

not just hunters
Vizslas are considered all-purpose dogs, as they are at home on land and in water. Their natural athleticism makes them fierce competitors in dog sports such as dock diving, agility, lure coursing, and barn hunts.

brains and beauty
As well as being beautiful dogs, vizslas are super intelligent. They are eager to please and highly trainable. They are also curious by nature, and owners should keep them occupied to prevent them from finding creative ways to get into trouble.

super-duper loyal
Vizslas are smart, gentle, and extremely affectionate. They are also well-mannered. Vizslas love their humans and require a large amount of interaction with them. Because of their devotion to their families, they make excellent watchdogs.

redheads
All vizslas have red coats and noses. Their hair is short and requires little maintenance. They don't have an insulating undercoat though, so they may get cold quickly when living in cold climates.

🐾 Paws for Thought 🐾
The vizsla was introduced to the United States in 1950 when a US State Department employee smuggled an adult dog and two puppies into the country from Hungary.

HOUND GROUP

The hound group is made up of sight hounds and scent hounds. While some members of the hound group may have abilities to chase and catch prey similar to dogs in the sporting group, a hound's strong nose and scent-tracking ability makes it unique. Hounds have an extremely strong prey drive and will stop at nothing until they catch what they are after. These dogs are often quite independent. They can be trained to hunt with their humans following along behind them on foot or horseback while the dogs track down their prey.

There are two types of hounds:

1 Scent hounds

2 Sight hounds

The borzoi is a large sight hound. It can reach speeds of up to 35 miles per hour (56 km/h). Originally bred to hunt wolves in Russia, this dog is known for its calm, agreeable temperament.

sporting group

hound group

working group

terrier group

toy group

non-sporting group

herding group

Scent Hounds

Scent hounds are tough, strong dogs that can walk and follow scents for long periods of time. They depend on their mighty noses to track anything from rabbits to missing people. Scent hounds have large, long ears that are used to funnel smells toward the nose as they are sniffing the ground. They also have large nasal cavities to help them better collect scents.

English Foxhound
These dogs were bred for the traditional British fox hunt, in which packs of foxhounds accompanied hunters on horseback across large fields, over hedges, and through streams in pursuit of foxes. English foxhounds have sturdy legs made for long runs, deep chests with plenty of lung power, and an amazing amount of endurance.

Black and Tan Coonhound
This hound is used to working the night shift! The black and tan coonhound was originally bred in the southern United States to hunt raccoons. They chased prey up trees and then howled for the hunter's attention. Black and tans' bravery, booming bark, and distinctive howl also made them useful for hunting bears, wolves, and cougars. These days, though, they are primarily used for hunting raccoons or as loyal companions.

Harrier
Harriers were bred from English foxhounds but are smaller in size. These two dogs are very similar in appearance. The harrier was bred for hunting rabbits and hares in the Middle Ages. Like other scent hounds, harriers require time outdoors each day to sniff and exercise.

Otterhound
The otterhound is one of the rarest breeds in the world. Otterhounds are known for their keen sense of smell and love of swimming. With their waterproof coats, broad shoulders, and webbed feet, they can swim for hours without getting tired. Meanwhile, they can track an otter's scent from the surface of the water while the otter swims below!

Bluetick Coonhound
Like other coonhound breeds, the bluetick was originally bred in the southern United States to hunt raccoons. This swift, high-energy breed has what raccoon hunters call a "cold nose." That's hunter lingo for the ability to follow a scent trail that is hours or even days old. The black and blue spots on the bluetick's coat is called ticking, which is where the dog's name comes from.

Beagle

Beagles are widely popular both as pets and as hunting dogs. They were originally bred to hunt rabbits and hares, but their incredible sense of smell makes them ideal for a variety of other jobs, too. You can find beagles working in airports as detection dogs, sniffing luggage for prohibited food items. Beagles' famous good nature and gentle temperament make them excellent therapy dogs as well.

tails up!
A thick tail with a white tip held upright helps alert hunters when the beagle is following a scent.

medium or large?
Beagles come in two sizes: those that are 13 inches (33 cm) or less at the shoulder, and those that are 13 to 15 inches (33–38 cm) at the shoulder.

follow your nose
Beagles have a very high prey drive. Once they catch a whiff of something, they will want to follow it. If you are keeping a beagle as a pet, you should make sure you always walk it on a leash and have your yard securely fenced. Check for any areas where a beagle could wriggle under or climb over. Yes, over! Beagles can be clever escapists when they are following their noses.

short legs
A beagle's short, sturdy legs help keep it low to the ground, where scents are easier to pick up.

sense of smell
Along with the bloodhound and the basset hound, the beagle has one of the best senses of smell in the canine world. A beagle has about 225 million scent receptors. In contrast, a dachshund has about 125 million.

long neck
A long neck helps the beagle drop its nose as close to the ground as possible.

so many sounds
Beagles make three distinct sounds: a regular bark, a howl, and a yodel-like sound called a bay that they use while hunting.

🐾 Paws for Thought 🐾
Snoopy from the *Peanuts* comic strip is a Beagle. The creator, Charles Schulz, based Snoopy on his own childhood dog.

Basset Hound

Despite their sad-looking, droopy faces, basset hounds are gentle, happy, easygoing dogs. They make excellent family pets, and while they are described as laid-back, they can also be stubborn. The basset hound is prized for its scenting ability, which is second only to the bloodhound's. Basset hounds were originally bred in France in the 1500s to hunt hares. The word *basset* comes from the French word *bas*, meaning "low."

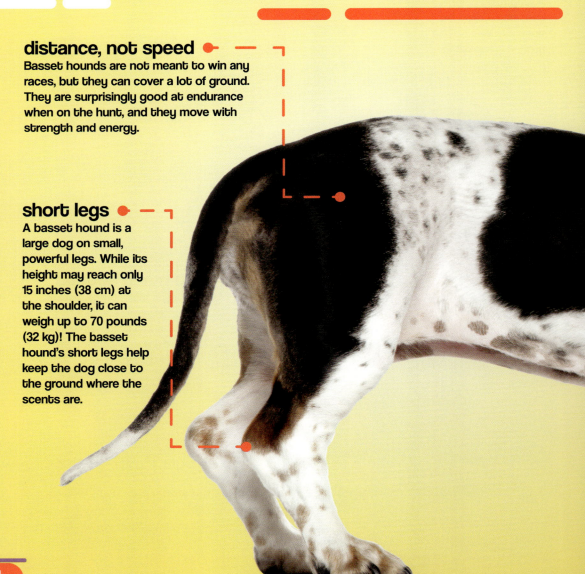

distance, not speed
Basset hounds are not meant to win any races, but they can cover a lot of ground. They are surprisingly good at endurance when on the hunt, and they move with strength and energy.

short legs
A basset hound is a large dog on small, powerful legs. While its height may reach only 15 inches (38 cm) at the shoulder, it can weigh up to 70 pounds (32 kg)! The basset hound's short legs help keep the dog close to the ground where the scents are.

droopy face
The droopy skin on a basset hound's face isn't just for good looks. It also helps trap scents and hold the smells close to the dog's nose.

super sniffer
A basset hound's large, cool, wet nose grabs and dissolves scent molecules from the air and brings them into the nose with each inhale.

built-in sweepers
The basset hound's long ears sweep scents from the ground toward the dog's powerful nose.

bark! bark!
Basset hounds have a loud, baying-like bark. They are known to be very vocal dogs.

🐾 Paws for Thought 🐾
A basset hound was used as the logo for a brand of shoes called Hush Puppies for so long that people started to refer to these dogs as Hush Puppies, too!

Bloodhound

The bloodhound has the most powerful sense of smell in the canine world. Originally bred for hunting more than 1,000 years ago, bloodhounds are now used around the globe to find lost or missing people and in search-and-rescue missions. Even with today's advanced technology, there isn't a scenting gadget invented that is more accurate than this breed's nose.

strong body
Don't let the bloodhound's loose suit fool you! Under all those folds is a large, muscular body.

powerful legs
Bloodhounds have long, strong legs built for walking great distances. Their noses can sometimes lead them over a variety of harsh terrain, and these dogs won't stop until they find what they are looking for.

face folds
A bloodhound's loose, moist jowls and droopy face help trap scent molecules and keep them around the dog's nose.

super snoot
A bloodhound can follow a scent trail that is more than a week old! This breed has more than 300 million scent receptors (for comparison, a human has just 5 million). Bloodhounds can follow a scent trail made up of skin cells, sweat, or even breath!

gentle giant
Male bloodhounds can weigh up to 110 pounds (50 kg) and stand up to 27 inches (69 cm) at the shoulder. Despite their size, they are gentle, patient, and affectionate dogs that make great pets.

strong shoulders
Bloodhounds' strong shoulders allow them to keep their heads down for long periods of time while sniffing the ground.

🐾 Paws for Thought 🐾
Have you ever wondered what kind of dog Goofy's pet Pluto is? A bloodhound! The character of Goofy himself is meant to resemble a bloodhound, too.

Treeing Walker Coonhound

The treeing walker coonhound was first bred in Virginia to hunt raccoons. These dogs hunt by chasing raccoons into trees, which is how they got their name. Walkers are "hot-nosed," which means that while hunting, they will leave a scent they're following if they find a fresher one. For hunters, this can mean a greater catch.

works well with others
Walkers can hunt alone or in packs. When working in packs, these courageous dogs have been known to hunt larger prey such as cougars and bobcats.

muscular hindquarters
Walkers have muscular hindquarters, which help them run fast and cover lots of ground while chasing prey.

different voices
The treeing walker uses different types of barks to signal to the hunter. They make a bugle-like noise while tracking so the hunter can follow them. Once they have a raccoon trapped up a tree, they will switch to a short, choppy bark.

personality
Walkers love their people! They are friendly, outgoing, and smart. They are also incredibly brave dogs.

dense coat
The walker's coat is short but dense. It provides protection from brush while out in rough terrain. Walkers can be black, white, or tricolored with a variety of markings.

🐾 Paws for Thought 🐾
Treeing walker coonhounds are good with kids and make great family pets.

Dachshund

Don't be fooled by this little dog's long, silly body and adorable good looks. Dachshunds were originally bred about 600 years ago to do underground battle with fierce badgers. And they were so good at it that their German name translates to "badger dog" in English. Although today's dachsies are no longer fighting underground, their confidence and feisty spirit lives on as a popular family pet!

long body
A dachsie's long, low-to-the-ground body was perfect for burrowing into a badger's den or into tight spaces where a badger may try to hide.

two sizes
Dachshunds come in two sizes: standard and miniature. Minis weigh 11 pounds (5 kg) or less, and standards weigh 16 to 32 pounds (7–15 kg).

many coats
Dachsies have three types of coats: smooth, longhaired, or wirehaired.

little legs
These short little legs keep dachshunds close to the ground where all the scents are. They also have wide, paddle-like feet to help push them along underground.

pack fighters
In addition to hunting badgers, packs of dachshunds would sometimes be used to hunt wild boars and wolverines.

loud bark
For a small dog, the dachsie has a big bark. All that noise serves a purpose. When the dog is underground and has found its prey, the bark tells the human hunter where it is.

deep chest
A dachshund has a large, deep chest and big lungs. This was to make sure the dog had enough endurance to fight underground for long periods of time.

🐾 Paws for Thought 🐾

The first official Olympic mascot was a dachshund named Waldi. Waldi debuted in Munich, Germany, for the 1972 Summer Olympics and was based on a dog owned by one of the organizers.

Sight Hounds

Sight hounds, also known as gazehounds, rely on their keen vision rather than their noses. They are sleek, long-legged running machines capable of explosive bursts of speed to chase down fast-moving prey such as hare or deer. All sight hounds have elongated heads with eyes that are placed far apart to give them excellent peripheral, or side, vision. They have slender waists and lean bodies.

Whippet

In the 1800s, coal miners in northern England enjoyed watching the popular sport of greyhound racing. The coal miners didn't have the money or the space to have expensive race dogs of their own, so their solution was to breed a smaller version of the greyhound. The result was the whippet, nicknamed "the poor man's racehorse." Whippets must be exercised regularly, but they are generally low-maintenance dogs.

Basenji

The basenji is known as the "barkless dog." Instead of barking, it makes a noise similar to a yodel. The basenji comes from Africa and is one of the oldest breeds. Its image is even believed to be depicted on some ancient Egyptian artifacts. Basenjis have keen eyesight and are capable of impressive bursts of speed like all sight hounds. They are also skilled scent hounds, making them members of both hound subgroups.

Sloughi

The sloughi (pronounced "sloo-ghee") is another ancient breed from North Africa. It is believed that sloughis were bred to hunt game such as foxes, jackals, and gazelles across difficult terrain. Like all sight hounds, they have a strong prey drive, so they must be leashed when on walks. If something catches their eye, they will be down the street before you realize they are gone!

Saluki

The saluki's history dates back 9,000 years to Asia and northern Africa. They were favorites of Egyptian pharaohs, Alexander the Great, and royal families of Asia. One look at the saluki's elegant features and graceful trot makes it easy to see why. Salukis are gentle and loving, and with enough daily exercise, they make excellent house dogs.

Scottish Deerhound

This majestic giant is one of the tallest of all the dog breeds. The Scottish deerhound stands 32 inches (81 cm) at the shoulder and can weigh up to 110 pounds (50 kg). But their slim size doesn't stop them from swiftly chasing down much heavier deer. Their shaggy, wiry coats protected their skin from sharp plants or twigs in the Scottish forests where they were bred to hunt.

Greyhound

Ancient Egyptians originally used the greyhound for coursing, or chasing, game over long distances. The greyhound's endurance, extraordinary speed, and natural prey drive have made this dog a favorite for thousands of years. As their popularity spread, greyhounds became the template for all other coursing hounds. As pets, greyhounds are very affectionate and loving. After getting enough daily exercise, they are content to snooze around the house.

airborne!
When a greyhound is running at top speed, it spends 75 percent of its time with all of its legs off the ground!

fuel the machine
Greyhounds burn so much energy that they need foods higher in calories than less-active breeds. Greyhounds require a high-quality, protein-rich diet so those calories don't just turn to fat.

hare feet
A greyhound's feet are shaped like a hare's. The middle toes are longer than the toes on the outside, so they appear longer than other dogs' feet. Greyhounds also have strong claws.

built for speed
A greyhound's body is built to run. Its aerodynamic shape sports a flexible spine that acts like a spring. Their long legs provide propulsion, and they can take huge strides. The dog's body is sleek with a narrow waist, creating little wind resistance.

heart and lungs

The greyhound's heart and lungs are large for the dog's size. This is to keep up with the amount of blood and oxygen the greyhound needs while racing at an incredible top speed of 45 miles per hour (72 km/h).

lookin' at you

Greyhounds have eyes placed far apart on their heads, giving them a 270-degree range of sight. They can also see about a half mile in front of them. They can detect the tiniest movement of their prey and be off in a flash.

🐾 Paws for Thought 🐾

The greyhound is the second-fastest land animal on Earth. The only animal that's faster is the cheetah, which can reach a top speed of 70 miles per hour (130 km/h) for short bursts.

Rhodesian Ridgeback

The regal Rhodesian ridgeback is known for more than the hair that gives it its name. These brave dogs were originally bred as a guard dogs and lion hunters! They used their superb hunting skills to help track lions over long distances, then secured them until hunters arrived. Today, ridgebacks are active, loving dogs that will join you on a jog, hike, or swim. They excel at dog sports like agility and lure coursing.

ridge and coat
The Rhodesian ridgeback has a distinctive line of hair down its back. Compared to the rest of the dog's coat, the ridge grows in the opposite direction. From the shoulders, the ridge of hair narrows until ending in two whorls on either side of the hips.

stick with me
Ridgebacks are followers and like to be where their humans are. However, they can also be strong-willed and independent.

body
Ridgebacks have strong, muscular bodies. These active dogs have great endurance and need plenty of exercise.

quiet type
If a ridgeback is barking, it means something is not quite right and should be investigated. These dogs are generally the strong, silent type.

🐾 Paws for Thought 🐾
When the ridgeback was originally developed in South Africa, farmers were breeding various purebred dogs such as greyhounds, mastiffs, and terriers with a wild, ridged dog called the Khoikhoi dog. Of the new dogs, the ridged ones proved to be the toughest on hunts, and that resulted in the Rhodesian ridgeback.

Irish Wolfhound

The Irish wolfhound is a true gentle giant. When standing on their back legs, they can reach heights of 6 feet (1.8 m) at the shoulder. Despite their size, Irish wolfhounds have a tame nature and calm presence. They were bred to hunt not only wolves, but also deer, elk, and wild boar. Their impressive size and muscular build made it possible for them to chase and take down such large prey.

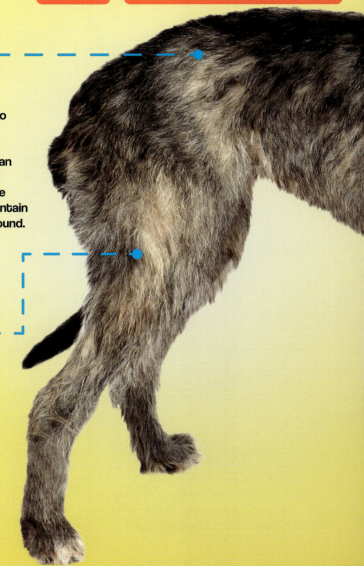

how big?!

The wolfhound stands up to 30 inches (76 cm) at the shoulder and can weigh 120 pounds (54 kg). Some can even get up to a whopping 180 pounds (82 kg). They are quite muscular but still maintain the sleek shape of a greyhound.

coat

The wolfhound has a wiry, water-resistant double coat to protect it from brush, harsh weather, and bites from prey. The soft undercoat keeps the dog snuggly warm. Wolfhounds are low maintenance and require brushing only once a week to remove dirt and loose hair.

personality
Beneath the wolfhound's scratchy coat is a kind, soft soul. They are well-known for their patient, friendly nature. They are also highly intelligent and make incredible family dogs.

eyes and facial hair
Wolfhounds have exceptional eyesight and will be off in a flash after their prey! The dog has extra-wiry hair over its eyes and a beard to protect its face while running through brush.

courageous in battle
Wolfhounds are considered an ancient breed, with a history that can be traced back 3,000 years. In addition to hunting, Irish wolfhounds were used as war dogs. In some battles, they would fight alongside their owners. In others, they would be sent in first to drag men off horses or chariots.

🐾 Paws for Thought 🐾
There is a saying among Irish wolfhound owners that goes back to the breed's history: "gentle when stroked, fierce when provoked." This saying refers to the wolfhound's legendary gentle personality and their ability to kill fierce fighters like wolves.

Pharaoh Hound

Pharaoh hounds were given their name because they resemble ancient Egyptian depictions of the god Anubis. But this breed is not known to come from Egypt at all. They were introduced to the Mediterranean island of Malta by the ancient Phoenicians, who came from what is now Lebanon. On Malta, these dogs were prized for their ability to hunt rabbits. From Malta they were introduced to England in the 1960s and quickly spread to the United States.

low maintenance
Considered to be "wash and wear" dogs, these hounds require very little grooming.

body and tail
Pharaoh hounds are smaller and lighter than greyhounds but have slightly heavier builds. Some have tails so long that they reach their ankles!

stunning face
When pharaoh hounds are happy or excited, their ears, noses, and cheeks turn a deeper shade of pink. They are sometimes called "blushing dogs." Their large, erect ears can swivel around to catch sound coming from different directions.

coloring
Pharaoh hounds have fur that is a light tan to a reddish-brown color. They lack pigments that give them any other coloring, which is why their noses are pink instead of black like most other dogs, and their eyes are amber colored.

so chill
Generally known for being calm and patient, pharaoh hounds can be a good choice as a pet for families with young children. These dogs tend to avoid strangers and are easily trained.

🐾 Paws for Thought 🐾
Unlike other sight hounds, which are fairly quiet, pharaoh hounds can be barky.

Afghan Hound

Everything about the Afghan hound seems to be slightly exaggerated, from its long and flowy coat to its pointy nose and fluffy feet. Afghan hounds are among the oldest of the purebred dogs. They can be traced back to what is now Afghanistan, Pakistan, and parts of India, where they were used for hunting on rocky mountain and desert terrains.

all in the hips
Afghan hounds have unique hips. Their hips are positioned higher than on other dogs and stick out. The hips are also wider apart than other dogs' hips, which allows them freedom to easily and swiftly maneuver over rocky landscapes.

fancy coat
The Afghan hound's long, silky coat protected the dog's skin from the harsh desert and mountain climates. As pets, they need frequent baths and regular brushing.

shock absorbers
Their huge paw pads acted as shock absorbers on harsh terrain.

vision
Like greyhounds, Afghan hounds have elongated faces and eyes that are set far apart.

brains and beauty
Although Afghan hounds may seem aloof, they are affectionate with their owners. They are strong-willed and bred to work independently.

activity
Afghan hounds need plenty of room to run at high speed when getting their daily activity in. If kept in a fenced-in yard, owners have to ensure that the fence is built high, because these dogs are good jumpers!

🐾 Paws for Thought 🐾
The Afghan hound's popularity soared in the United States after the makers of Barbie toys introduced her pet dog Beauty in 1979.

WORKING GROUP

Weighing in at over 70 pounds (32 kg), dogs that make up the working group are the largest and strongest of all the breeds. They are athletic, intelligent, and protective. They are also some of the world's oldest breeds. All dogs in the working group were bred to help humans in some way, whether guarding, pulling heavy loads, or performing rescues. Many dogs in the working group are still used to do these tasks today. Owners must be prepared to properly train a working dog if they want to keep one as a pet. They are generally determined and have strong personalities, which can be a lot to handle for first-time dog owners.

This gentle, affectionate dog is the Newfoundland. It can weigh up to 150 pounds (68 kg) and stand 28 inches (71 cm) at the shoulder. These dogs were originally used on fishing boats to haul nets and carts of fish. They're also excellent swimmers, and they frequently rescued grown men from drowning when they fell overboard.

- sporting group
- hound group
- working group
- terrier group
- toy group
- non-sporting group
- herding group

Doberman Pinscher

The Doberman pinscher is a newer dog breed that has only been around for about 150 years. In the 1880s, a German tax collector named Karl Friedrich Louis Dobermann wanted a dog he could use as protection while collecting money. He selected a combination of breeds to create what he thought would be a good guard dog. No one knows the exact combination of dogs he chose, but the result was the fiercely protective and loyal Doberman.

coat
A Doberman's coat can be red, black, blue, or fawn with rust-colored markings on the face, chest, legs, and paws. These short-haired dogs are average shedders and require little brushing.

work and play
Although still favored as guard dogs, Dobermans aren't all work and no play. A pet Doberman would gladly serve as your swimming or running buddy. They are powerful and energetic and like to play.

comparison
Dobermans are often compared to another popular guard dog, the rottweiler. While both are considered medium- to large-sized dogs, Dobermans are slightly taller and have a more slender build than the huskier rottweiler.

brains
Fearless and alert, Dobermans are very intelligent and capable of learning difficult tasks. They are easy to train and form close bonds with their family.

good looks
The German word *pinscher* means "terrier" in English. Dobermans are not terriers but got that part of their name from the German pinscher, which was used in the creation of the breed. Other dogs that may have been added to the mix include rottweilers, Weimaraners, and short-haired shepherds.

🐾 Paws for Thought 🐾
During World War II (1939–1945), the US army trained Dobermans as scouts to locate enemies and help soldiers avoid snipers. Doberman owners across the United States donated their family pets to serve alongside family members fighting in the war.

Rottweiler

The rottweiler's name comes from a town in Germany, but this breed's history can be traced back to the armies of ancient Rome. Descended from big, strong mastiffs, the rottweiler's ancestors were used to protect the army's livestock as they moved from place to place. Left behind in Germany, these dogs evolved into the breed well-known today for its watchful, territorial, and protective nature, with a whole lot of devotion for its humans mixed in.

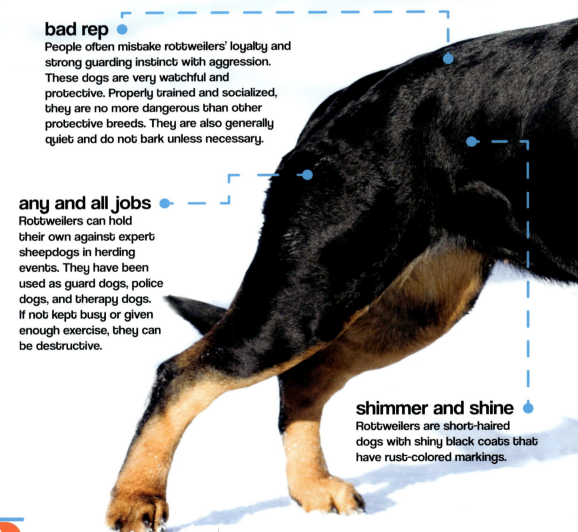

bad rep
People often mistake rottweilers' loyalty and strong guarding instinct with aggression. These dogs are very watchful and protective. Properly trained and socialized, they are no more dangerous than other protective breeds. They are also generally quiet and do not bark unless necessary.

any and all jobs
Rottweilers can hold their own against expert sheepdogs in herding events. They have been used as guard dogs, police dogs, and therapy dogs. If not kept busy or given enough exercise, they can be destructive.

shimmer and shine
Rottweilers are short-haired dogs with shiny black coats that have rust-colored markings.

watch out for drool!
Rottweilers' "loose lips" mean that they tend to drool. They are also known as leaners and rest their bodies against people's legs. This trait is thought to come from when they were cattle drivers and used their body weight to push cattle in the direction they wanted them to go.

loyal
As well as being loyal protectors, rottweilers are confident and can be a bit stubborn. Because of their size and strength, training needs to begin when they are small puppies.

🐾 Paws for Thought 🐾
In Germany, rottweilers are sometimes referred to as "butchers' dogs." This is because butchers used them to haul carts of meat to customers and would even tie their money around the dogs' necks to deter thieves.

Mastiff

Mastiffs are the heaviest dog breed. A full-grown male mastiff can weigh more than 200 pounds (91 kg). That's as much as a baby elephant! Mastiffs are also strong and muscular—so much so that the ancient Romans pitted them in fights against bears, lions, and gladiators. Today, this ancient breed has lost some of its fight, but mastiffs still make good guard dogs.

activity level
For people looking for large, protective dogs, mastiffs require less exercise than other protective breeds. They still need about an hour of exercise per day and would not turn down the chance to play with a tug toy.

body
Mastiffs are only slightly smaller than the tallest breeds. They are exceptionally strong and heavy-boned dogs. Their bodies are rectangular shaped, and their heads are large and wide. Their coats can be fawn, apricot, or brindle striped.

calm presence
Mastiffs make excellent therapy dogs because of their loving, gentle, and loyal character.

loose skin
The face folds on mastiffs helped keep important parts safe when they were fighting. But their loose jowls mean they are also excessive droolers.

slow growers
Mastiffs take a long time to mature because of their size. They aren't considered mentally and physically mature until they are about three years old. So, it's important to start training mastiffs when they are young. You wouldn't want to wait until they are bigger and stronger than you!

🐾 Paws for Thought 🐾
Zorba the mastiff holds the world record for being the heaviest dog ever at 343 pounds (156 kg). He weighed as much as a refrigerator!

Great Dane

Great Danes come from Germany, where they were bred to hunt wild boar. They were also used by members of the nobility as guard dogs. They are the national dog of Germany, where they are called *Deutsche Dogge*, or "German mastiff." Today, the Great Dane is a popular choice for families who want a dog for protection—its size alone is often enough to scare off any intruders.

activity
Great Danes need to exercise at least twice a day. They are good at dog sports such as agility, flyball, and obedience.

choose a color
Great Danes have seven different coat colors and patterns, including brindle (yellow-gold hair mixed with black stripes), harlequin (a black and white patchwork pattern like the one shown here), and merle (gray with black spots). Others are solid colors, such as blue (gray), black, or fawn with a black face "mask" and eyebrows. Great Danes that have mantle coats are black on the upper half and white on the lower half, including the underbelly.

flappy lips
Some Great Danes drool more than others. The drool is caused by their flappy lips. The flaps create pockets that catch the drool until it overflows.

tie for tallest
Great Danes are tied with Irish wolfhounds as the tallest dogs. When standing on their hind legs, Great Danes are taller than most people!

too close for comfort
Great Danes are usually social and friendly dogs. They are highly affectionate with their family members. They are way too big to be lap dogs, but that doesn't stop some Great Danes. They may try to sit on your lap in an attempt to be closer to you!

🐾 Paws for Thought 🐾
The characters Scooby-Doo and Marmaduke are two of the most famous Great Danes in popular culture.

Boxer

Boxers originated in Germany in the late 1800s. No one knows for sure how they got their name, but some people say it comes from the way they stand on their hind legs and hit with their front paws during fights. Boxers came from a larger breed called the bullenbeisser, which was used for hunting wild boar. When hunting wild boar went out of fashion, these dogs were crossbred with bulldogs and Great Danes to create the smaller, sleeker-shaped boxer. Despite their name, boxers are better known as service dogs than they are as fighters.

boxers as service dogs

Boxers are alert, sensitive, and in-tune with people. This makes them great alert dogs for people with epilepsy. A boxer bonds with a person who has epilepsy and can sense oncoming seizures by responding to subtle changes in the person's behavior.

training

Boxers get bored easily and need consistent training, socialization, and exercise.

flashy flash

Boxers have a smooth, tight coat that can be fawn or brindle colored. They have white markings called "flash" on their underbellies, feet, necks, and faces.

flat-faced
A boxer's lower jaw sticks out farther than its top jaw, which gives the dog what is called an "undershot jaw" or "underbite." Combined with its skin folds and short muzzle, the boxer's face has a distinctive pushed-in look.

zzzzzzzz
You might want to think twice about owning a boxer if you want a dog that will sleep with you at night. Boxers snore!

🐾 Paws for Thought 🐾
Boxers were used as "casualty dogs" during World War I (1914–1918). After battles, they would help soldiers who were alive but injured on the battlefield. If a soldier was dying, the boxer would stay with him and give him comfort until the end.

Cane Corso

The large, mastiff-style ancestors of the cane corso were brought from Greece to Italy in ancient times, and the Romans bred them with dogs native to Italy. One of the earliest jobs of the cane corso was in war. The Roman army sent them into enemy territory with buckets of flaming oil strapped to their backs. Later they were used for hunting wild boar, driving livestock, and guarding property. Fearless and powerful, loyal and devoted, their name means "bodyguard dog" in Latin.

coats
The corso has a short, stiff coat that comes in black, gray, fawn, black brindle, gray brindle, red, chestnut, and brindle.

busy is better
These powerful, muscular dogs have large heads and mouths. They are active and driven, and they require intense daily exercise that challenges them not only physically but mentally as well. They perform well in dog sports that involve tracking, agility, and scent work.

training is important
The cane corso is smart but sensitive. They do not respond well to being yelled at. Instead, they need an owner who is patient, calm, and consistent with their training. Even when grown, these dogs benefit from daily obedience drills. But the reward for an owner who can properly train a cane corso is a very devoted and protective pet.

roo-roo!
The corso is a vocal dog. It communicates using barks, howls, snuffles, and snorts. It also makes a "roo-roo" sound.

loyal friend
Although known for its loyalty, the corso is also assertive and willful. You could even say it's a bit on the bossy side. These dogs will take the upper hand if allowed to. Training is a must from the start to establish who will be pack leader—owner or dog!

🐾 Paws for Thought 🐾
These dogs are naturally suspicious of people they don't know and are said to be constantly on patrol.

Bernese Mountain Dog

Bernese mountain dogs come from a region of Switzerland called Bern, which is known for its pastures and farms. This breed performed many different tasks on farms, such as guiding and guarding livestock, but it was especially valued for its ability to pull carts that weighed many times more than its own body. Before people had machinery to help with tasks, Bernese mountain dogs contributed greatly to the success of family farms.

so. much. fur.
All Bernese mountain dogs have long, silky tricolor coats (black, white, and rust) with distinctive markings. The undercoat is woolly for warmth. Berners shed a lot and need weekly brushing.

how big?!
Berners are sturdy, powerful, and built for work. Their broad hindquarters provide strength. They are up to 28 inches (70 cm) tall and weigh up to 115 pounds (52 kg).

hitch 'em up!
If you hitch a Bernese mountain dog up to a sleigh or wagon, the dog will pull it. This makes a nice treat for families with young children. Berners are also good companions on hikes and walks. They need at least a half-hour of exercise each day.

family friend
Berners make excellent pets for families with children. They are sweet, affectionate dogs.

training
Like all large, powerful dogs, Berners grow quickly. Both owners and pets benefit from training them when they are still small.

brrrr
Berners thrive doing cold-weather outdoor activities and even like to romp in the snow!

🐾 Paws for Thought 🐾
Bernese mountain dog clubs across North America host "drafting" events, which test this breed's natural ability to control, maneuver, and pull a cart over hills and across different terrain.

Saint Bernard

The origin of the Saint Bernard goes something like this: Nearly 1,000 years ago, in a place called the Great St. Bernard Pass high in the Swiss Alps, a group of monks built a shelter for travelers. There, the monks developed the Saint Bernard breed as a working dog to pull carts filled with supplies and to rescue travelers lost in the snow. Whether or not this origin story is true doesn't change the fact that these dogs were certainly used for drafting and for search-and-rescue in the mountains of Switzerland.

hairy both ways
Saint Bernards have either long or short coats, but either way their coats are dense, and they shed twice a year. The long-coated type has longer, wavy hair. Many have dark-haired "masks" around their eyes.

activity level
Saint Bernards don't require a lot of exercise compared to other breeds, but they do require doing things with you and don't like being left on their own for long periods of time.

look at that face!
Saint Bernards have big heads and large, powerful bodies. Their wrinkly foreheads, deep-set eyes, and black face markings give them lovable, dopey-looking faces. But watch out for drool!

calm and cuddly
Saint Bernards are known for their calm and gentle manner. They are sometimes used as therapy dogs.

be careful, puppy
Like other large working breeds, Saint Bernards are slow to reach maturity but are strong and powerful at an early age. As they grow, owners have to take care that the puppies do not run too much or bulk up too fast, as it can harm their growing bones and joints. As adults, they can weigh up to 180 pounds (82 kg), and they grow up to 30 inches (76 cm) tall at the shoulder.

🐾 Paws for Thought 🐾
Saint Bernards often worked as pairs in avalanche rescue missions. After digging someone out of the snow, one dog would go get help, while the other would stay with the lost person and lay on top of them to keep them warm until help arrived!

Siberian Husky

Siberian huskies have been used as arctic sled dogs for at least 2,000 years. The Siberian husky is often confused with the Alaskan Malamute, but the key to these two dogs' origins is in their names. Siberian huskies originated in Siberia, the Arctic region of northern Asia. The Alaskan Malamute was bred by the Malimiut Indigenous people of Alaska. These breeds are just two examples of the several types of Arctic dogs.

coat
Siberian huskies have thick double coats that shed twice a year. While they do require frequent brushing, these dogs don't need to be bathed often and have very little odor.

long-distance runners
Siberian huskies are smaller than Alaskan Malamutes. The people of the Arctic who originally bred Siberian huskies needed sled dogs that could carry light loads over very long distances. Malamutes were bred to carry heavier loads over shorter distances.

tough paws
Siberian huskies needed to have tough, thickly cushioned paw pads for long-distance running in extreme conditions. They have a lot of fur between their toes, so they look like they're wearing fuzzy slippers!

family dog
Siberian huskies do not make good watchdogs and are not protective. They will, however, attach to all family members equally rather than choosing a favorite.

look into my eyes
Siberian huskies can have brown or blue eyes. Some huskies have one of each color, or even both colors in the same eye!

escape artists
Pet owners need to constantly be aware of the Siberian husky's urge to run. At home, huskies need to be watched and kept in a secure, fenced-in yard when left outside alone. Even fenced in, these dogs are clever escape artists.

born to run
The natural instinct of a Siberian husky is to get out and run . . . and then run some more. They aren't the fastest runners, but they do have incredible endurance.

🐾 Paws for Thought 🐾

In 1925, a dog-team relay involving 20 mushers, or sled-team drivers, and 150 sled dogs traveled more than 670 miles (1,078 km). They brought life-saving medicine to the people of Nome, Alaska, during a disease outbreak. The stars of the journey were two Siberian huskies named Balto and Togo.

Anatolian Shepherd

The Anatolian shepherd originated in what is now the country of Türkiye. These dogs were bred to be large and imposing to scare predators away from sheep and goats. They're still used to protect livestock, and one look at the size of this dog is often all it takes for a potential predator to change its mind. The Anatolian shepherd will fight if needed but prefers to use the intimidation factor to its advantage.

weatherproof
The Anatolian plateau, where these dogs came from, has hot summers and cold winters. The Anatolian shepherd's thick undercoat protects the dog from the elements and sheds twice a year. This coat helps the dog stay warm while guarding its flock on bitter-cold nights.

how big?!
Definitely one of the largest dog breeds, Anatolian shepherds are 29 inches (74 cm) from ground to shoulder. They are hardy and rugged dogs with heavy heads.

ready to roam
Not lazy, but not overly active, the Anatolian shepherd does well living in places where it has space to roam. For pet owners, this means a big backyard is better than apartment living.

woof! woof!
In addition to using their size as defense, they have a loud bark that scares predators away.

flock before friends
Anatolian shepherds focus on their flock over anything else. They are so independent that they can take care of the flock on their own, without needing a human handler around. Without livestock to care for, Anatolian shepherds will become loyal to their human families but remain wary of strangers.

🐾 Paws for Thought 🐾
Farmers in the African country of Namibia use Anatolian shepherds to protect their livestock from cheetahs! Even a cheetah knows enough not to challenge these dogs.

More Working Dogs

Akita
Akitas are large dogs bred in Japan. They're used as guard dogs and for hunting bears.

Alaskan Malamute
Incredibly strong, these sled dogs are able to run long distances.

Boerboel
The boerboel is a South African dog bred to be a guard dog on farms.

Dogue de Bordeaux
This French breed is muscular and powerful, similar to the mastiff.

Great Pyrenees
This massive, thick-coated dog was originally bred to guard livestock from wolves and other predators on mountaintops.

Greater Swiss Mountain Dog
The greater Swiss mountain dog originated in the Swiss Alps and was used to pull carts of meat and dairy to market from farms.

Komondor
Also called the Hungarian sheepdog, the komondor is a large dog with a corded coat. It was bred to guard livestock.

Leonberger
These large dogs of German origin were bred as watchdogs and to pull carts on farms.

Portuguese Water Dog
Originally bred to work with fishers retrieving broken or lost equipment, this dog could also herd fish into nets and swim ship-to-ship delivering messages!

Samoyed
The medium-sized Samoyed was used to haul sleds, herd reindeer, and keep their owners warm at night by sleeping on them! They can move a sled one and a half times their weight.

TERRIER GROUP

For a dog to be considered a terrier, it must have been bred to find and root out vermin and hunt small prey. Many of these dogs were kept on farms and used to protect barns and livestock from rats and other pests. The word *terrier* comes from the Latin word *terra*, meaning "earth." They were given this name because they will dig or burrow underground to find and catch their prey. Terriers are usually described as active, feisty, and spirited dogs!

There are three types of terriers:

1 Short-legged

2 Long-legged

3 Bull-type

Miniature schnauzers were originally bred as "ratters," or to catch rats. There are two larger version of schnauzers—the standard and the giant—which are in the working dog group rather than the terrier group. Miniature schnauzers are great family pets and excel at dog sports.

- sporting group
- hound group
- working group
- **terrier group**
- toy group
- non-sporting group
- herding group

Short-Legged

These short-legged, long-bodied dogs often worked underground to find their prey. With small, flexible bodies, they were able to follow prey headfirst into underground dens or burrows. Their feet point outward so that when they dig to enlarge the hole in the earth, the dirt gets thrown to the side, out of their way. Many of these breeds have long hair on their faces, which served as protection while fighting rats or other vermin. A snapping rodent would end up with a mouthful of hair rather than piercing the dog's skin.

Cesky Terrier
There are only about 600 Cesky (pronounced "chess-key") terriers living in the United States. They were originally bred to hunt hare and fox in Czechoslovakia. They stand just 13 inches (33 cm) tall at the shoulder. Despite their small size, Ceskys make for fierce competitors in dog sports like agility and tracking.

Skye Terrier

Standing only 10 inches (25 cm) at the shoulder, the Skye terrier can be twice as long as it is tall. Skyes were bred in the 1600s by Scottish farmers to control the fox and badger population. Badgers are fierce adversaries with sharp teeth and razor-like claws, but they were no sweat for the Skye terrier. In the 1800s, Queen Victoria became a fan of the breed, and the Skye terrier's popularity went from working farm dog to a popular choice among the nobility.

Dandie Dinmont Terrier

The Dandie Dinmont terrier has a unique look. Its front legs are shorter than the back legs. The dog has a large head, big, soulful eyes, a long body . . . and then there's that hair! Dandies may be small, but they have a big, baritone bark. They were built this way on purpose. They had some fierce prey to hunt: otters and badgers.

Cairn Terrier

This tiny, tenacious dog is the cairn terrier. Originally used as farm dogs, cairns did battle with formidable opponents such as otters, foxes, rats, and other small vermin. These teeny terrors—er, terriers—would dive headfirst into piles of rocks, or cairns, which were used as road markers or memorials. From there, the dogs would fight their foes or dig their way underground to flush them out. Today, cairn terriers make loyal and lovable family pets.

tiny package, big attitude
Cairns are small and light. Standing just 10 inches (25 cm) from the floor to the top of the shoulder, and weighing just 14 pounds (6 kg), the dog's small size was vital for squeezing into rocky passages, dens, or burrows.

coat
The cairn sports a weatherproof double coat. The outside is wiry and keeps water and dirt from getting to the skin. The inside is woolly and warm.

braveheart
Cairn terriers are confident little dogs. They are bold and courageous. These are qualities they would have needed to fight menacing opponents, and they continue to have those qualities today. They seem unaware they are the smallest dog in the waiting room at the vet.

foot facts
Cairns must dig! Their brains are wired for it, and their feet are built for it. Their front feet are larger than their back feet for maximum dirt grab-ability, as well as being padded for protection. They also come equipped with strong nails to help them dig and for defense.

what big teeth you have
Cairns have large teeth for such small dogs. They would have needed them to fight foxes and badgers.

bossy boots
Cairn terriers can be very assertive. That's a nice way of saying they can be bossy. Owners should start training early and be consistent. You'll need to show this little dog who's in charge . . . or else it might not be you!

🐾 Paws for Thought 🐾

The movie *The Wizard of Oz* was released in 1939, and audiences were introduced to Toto, a cairn terrier. The breed quickly rose in popularity.

Scottish Terrier

Is any face as instantly recognizable? That grizzled beard, the adorable eyebrows, and the jaunty walk can only belong to the Scottish terrier! These are hardy little workers, bred to help fight the rodent infestation that was threatening grain storages and carrying diseases in the Scottish Highlands. They were also used to hunt rabbits, otters, foxes, and badgers.

playtime and more play
They may not look like it, but Scotties are high-energy dogs. In fact, they have earned the nickname "little diehard." Start a game of fetch with one and you'll quickly find out why—you'll quit playing before they do! Scotties need a good walk and a solid bout of playtime every day. With enough activity to meet their needs they are well suited for living in a small home or apartment.

grooming
Regular grooming is needed to keep the traditional Scottie cut with eyebrows, beard, and mustache looking their best. Weekly brushings are also needed to keep the coat tangle free. Scotties have wiry topcoats and dense, soft undercoats. They come in black, brindle, and wheaten yellow.

little legs
At only 10 inches (25 cm) tall and weighing 22 pounds (10 kg), this dog may be small, but it's solidly built. Scotties' strong little legs are made for digging and carrying them over the craggy Scottish Highlands.

manners
Scotties are quite wary of new people until they get to know them. They are also territorial, but this makes them good watchdogs. Socialization and training from a young age is important so they can learn good manners.

that face!
The facial hair isn't just a style choice—the eyebrows, beard, and mustache protected the Scottie's face from bites while in pursuit of vermin. An opponent would get a mouthful of hair if it tried to take a bite of the dog's face.

what'd you say?
Scotties can be quite barky!

🐾 Paws for Thought 🐾
According to a poll in 2017, the Scottish terrier is the most popular Monopoly game piece. The game maker, Hasbro, gave people the chance to pick their favorite piece from 64 options. Of the 4.3 million votes cast, the most were for the Scottie!

West Highland Terrier

The West Highland terrier, or Westie for short, is among the most popular of the short-legged terriers. Westies can trace their Scottish roots back to the 1700s. These hardy little workers and a few other breeds (the cairn, Scottish, Skye, and Dandie Dinmont terriers) were developed to help fight rodent infestations. Seems like a pretty big job for a bunch of little terriers, but the Westies were up to the task!

built-in handle
The Westie has a sturdy, carrot-shaped tail that was sometimes used to pull the dog out from underground burrows if it got stuck. However, it's never advisable to pull a dog's tail, as there are nerves in the spine that can be damaged.

snowy white armor
A Westie's white fur is no accident. White fur was highly visible and kept Westies from being mistaken for the prey they were hunting. Their tough, dense coats protected them while pushing through bramble. The double coat requires grooming every four to six weeks to maintain the Westie haircut (the hair on the dog's head, belly, and legs is left longer).

body
Westies' compact bodies are built for digging and pushing themselves into the ground after their prey. They have larger front feet to help throw as much dirt as possible, powerful rear feet to push themselves forward, and small bodies to wedge into the holes they make.

happy and headstrong
Westies are independent and confident little dogs. They have a light-hearted and happy nature but are protective of their homes and families.

mouth
The Westie is vocal and has a loud bark for a dog so small. The Westie also has large teeth for a dog its size, but they came in handy for catching vermin.

digging
A Westie's digging and hunting instinct is strong, and many will do it in their backyards. Westies will chase anything that moves, so owners must make sure they're on a leash while out on walks.

🐾 Paws for Thought 🐾
March 20 is National Westie Day. It is the anniversary of the death of Edward Donald Malcolm, 16th Laird of Poltalloch, who is credited with developing the breed.

Russell Terrier

If you've watched TV or been to the movies, you've probably seen this adorable face. The Russell terrier (previously known as the Jack Russell terrier) has been everywhere! But there's so much more to these intelligent, super-friendly dogs than tricks. Russell terriers were originally developed by Reverend John Russell in the 1800s to bolt, or flush out, foxes from their dens. The hunting and digging instinct is strong in Russells and can't be trained out. Any small animal is prey, and they are always up for a chase.

born athletes
Russells are extremely athletic, agile, and fast. Their natural abilities mean they need lots of physical activity. They can get up to mischief if they have energy to burn and no outlet. They also love to dig! Owners will often find them "helping" with the gardening. Russells are outstanding competitors at agility and flyball.

wardrobe options
Russells have three types of coats: smooth, rough, and broken. Smooth coats are short, dense hairs. Rough coats are made up of coarse, straight, longer hair. A broken coat is a combination of both smooth and rough coats. All Russells are white with tan markings.

legs or springs?
Russells can jump as high as 5 feet (1.5 m). That's four times their own height. They are also excellent climbers. Needless to say, make sure the dog is in a fenced area before taking off its leash!

body
Russells have small chests that were made to fit into the holes they dug. Their flexible bodies allowed them to maneuver underground to follow their prey.

keen sniffer
In the 1940s, the brown tree snake accidentally made its way onto the island of Guam, a US territory. The invasive species posed a threat to Guam's delicate ecosystem. The US Department of Agriculture used specially trained Russell terriers to find the snakes and prevent them from getting into outgoing cargo to other islands in the Pacific, where they could disturb other ecosystems. Russells' scent abilities, high energy, and hunting instincts made them a good fit for the job.

🐾 Paws for Thought 🐾
Russell terriers' extreme trainability makes them natural TV and movie stars! They can easily be trained to do tricks and perform commands on cue, so naturally they took those skills to Hollywood!

Long-Legged

Unlike their short-legged cousins, long-legged terriers work more like above-ground exterminators. The terriers in this subgroup prefer to dig out vermin rather than burrowing into the ground or squeezing themselves into holes or dens to search for them. As the name suggests, these terriers have long legs. Their feet face directly forward, so that when the dogs are digging, dirt gets thrown under their bodies, through their back legs, and out of the way.

American Hairless Terrier
The American hairless terrier was developed in Louisiana. When a hairless is born, it is usually covered in fine hair, which falls out as the dog gets older. They can sometimes have eyebrows and whiskers as adults. If you own a hairless terrier, you will have to make sure to protect it from sunburn in hot weather, and keep it warm in cold weather.

Manchester Terrier
In the mid-1800s, Manchester, England, relied heavily on its textile trade. Unfortunately, the textile factories had rat problems. Breeders worked on coming up with a dog that could get rid of the rats but was also super fast. That way, the dogs could also be used to hunt rabbits. Thus, the Manchester terrier was born, solving both of these problems!

Kerry Blue Terrier

The Kerry blue terrier gets its name from its coat. The "blue" color can range from a deep, slate blue to a light blue-gray. Kerry is the area in Ireland where they were originally from. These muscular farm dogs are energetic, loving, and alert. They stand 20 inches (51 cm) at the shoulder and can weigh up to 40 pounds (18 kg).

Bedlington Terrier

Don't be fooled by the Bedlington terrier's strange haircut. In the 1800s, these gentle, lamb-looking dogs were fierce vermin killers working in coal mines in Bedlington, England. The ridge of hair down the dog's face was to protect its eyes from rat bites, and the pom-poms on the ears were to stop rats from latching on. Today, Bedlingtons are playful, loving companion dogs.

Airedale

Sometimes called the "king of the terriers," the Airedale is the largest breed in the terrier group. Their name comes from the area in northern England where they were first bred as ratters. Not only are these dogs bred from the otterhound and several types of terriers, they also have some setter, retriever, and herding dog mixed in. As a result, Airedales are one of the most versatile, multipurpose breeds. There's nothing these dogs can't do!

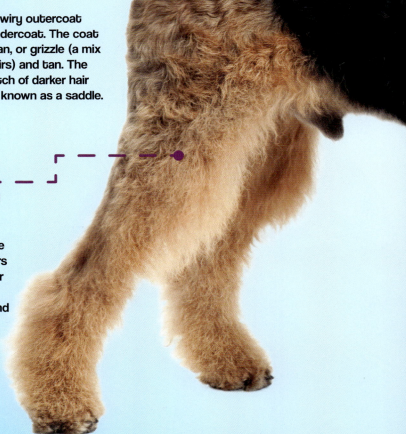

saddleback
The Airedale has a wiry outercoat and a soft, curly undercoat. The coat can be black and tan, or grizzle (a mix of red and black hairs) and tan. The dog has a large patch of darker hair on its back that is known as a saddle.

tall for a terrier
Airedales are medium-sized dogs and can be up to 23 inches (58 cm) tall at the shoulder. They have the high energy of other terriers but in a bigger package. For this reason, it's important that they have playtime and several walks a day.

long head
Airedales have long heads, beards, and eyebrows.

button ears
The ears of an Airedale are folded over halfway. This type of dog ear is sometimes called a button ear.

personality
Airedales are fearless and outgoing. They do not tire easily. They can also be determined and stubborn.

all-purpose
Because of their background, Airedales can be used for any number of jobs, such as hunting, herding, and guarding. They are a good choice for people looking for an active dog that can do a little bit of everything.

🐾 Paws for Thought 🐾

During World War I (1914–1918), Airedales were used as messenger dogs to carry notes to soldiers. They were also used as police dogs in Great Britain.

Soft-Coated Wheaten Terrier

One thing that sets the wheaten terrier apart from other terriers is its single-layered coat of soft hair instead of the stiff, wiry outercoat of many other breeds in the terrier group. In Ireland, where they originated, wheaten terriers were popular as all-purpose dogs on small farms. Irish law in the 1600s forbid peasant farmers from owning hounds, beagles, greyhounds, and spaniels—breeds reserved for the upper class. This meant wheatens were used not only to control the vermin population on farms but also as herders, watchdogs, and hunting dogs.

wheat-colored adult
As puppies, wheatens' coats are dark brown. As they get older, their hair turns white and then the pale beige color that the adult wheaten is known for.

waves of silk
Wheatens don't shed much. Instead, they need daily brushing to remove excess hair. A wheaten's coat is slightly wavy and silky to the touch.

chasing instinct
Wheatens are smart, strong-willed dogs that like to chase things. This combination can make them challenging to train.

darker spots
Wheatens' muzzles and ears are slightly darker than the rest of their coat.

peek-a-boo
The lock of long hair that covers the wheaten's eyes is called a fall. Wheatens also have long, full beards.

a friendly warning
Wheatens make better watchdogs than guard dogs. Because they are alert and friendly, they will bark to let you know someone has arrived, but they are not likely to give much protection.

🐾 Paws for Thought 🐾
Wheaten dog owners refer to the bouncy greeting that wheatens give them as "the wheaten greetin'." That's because these dogs get jumpy when they are excited.

Rat Terrier

The rat terrier was recognized as a breed by the American Kennel Club in 2012. The development of this American breed began when British immigrants brought over terriers to be used in ratbaiting. Over time, these ratters were bred with faster breeds such as greyhounds, and with beagles for their pack-hunting mentality. Rat terriers were one of the most common farm dogs in the United States for controlling rats and rabbits, which would eat farm crops. Their popularity declined in the 1950s when chemical rat poison began to be used instead of the ratters, but they have made a comeback in recent years as sports dogs and service dogs.

piebald pattern
Rat terriers have smooth, shiny white coats that have piebald spotting, which means they have large patches of one or more colors.

standard and mini
Rat terriers come in two different sizes: standard and miniature. Standards can be up to 18 inches (46 cm) tall, while miniatures are 10 to 13 inches (24–33 cm) high.

trainable
Rat terriers are high-energy dogs, but they're calmer than many others in the terrier group.

what's up
Rat terriers have large ears that stand up when they are alert. Some rat terriers have ears that are always erect, while others are tipped (just the tip is folded over) or button ears (half erect and half folded).

playtime
One of the favorite activities of rat terriers is a game of fetch. As former ratters, they have a high prey drive and love the thrill of the chase.

diggers
Like many terrier breeds, rat terriers are known to be diggers.

🐾 Paws for Thought 🐾

In Europe in the Middle Ages, people had jobs as rat-catchers. Rat-catchers sometimes traveled from town to town with dogs known as ratters to help them in their work. Rats were a big problem because they spread disease and damaged food supplies.

Bull-Type

This small subgroup of terriers has a grisly past. These breeds from the 1700s and 1800s were bred for blood sport. In bullbaiting, a pack of bull-type terriers were pitted against a bull in a fight. In bearbaiting, they fought a bear. In dogfights, they fought each other. In ratbaiting, the dogs were put in a pen with rats to see how many they could kill. Spectators bet money on the outcome of these events, which always resulted in a bloody death for one or more of the animals. Despite their gruesome beginnings, bull-type terriers have been transformed into sweet, loving pets. Some of their more positive original traits remain, such as their well-developed, muscular bodies and fiery terrier spirit!

Miniature Bull Terrier

While they may look like miniature versions of the bull terrier, miniature bull terriers are their own breed. Soon after the standard bull terrier was developed in the 1830s, breeders developed the mini to be used as above-ground ratters (as opposed to other terriers that dig to find rats). Minis were used in small spaces where the larger bull terriers couldn't fit. Minis are highly energetic with larger-than-life personalities. They make excellent companion dogs but require a lot of patience.

American Staffordshire Terrier

The American Staffordshire terrier is the taller, heavier version of its cousin, the Staffordshire bull terrier. Staffordshire terriers arrived in the United States from England in the mid-1800s. Breeders began developing a larger, more laid-back version, which is now recognized as a separate breed—the American Staffordshire terrier. This loyal, good-natured breed requires training and socialization from an early age to ensure good canine manners.

Bull Terrier

If there was a dog show competition for the personality category, the bull terrier would take home "Best in Show." These dogs are the mischievous, comical geniuses of the dog world, and their distinctive "egghead" shape just adds to this image. Originally developed to be champions in dogfights, this slick, muscular breed was adopted as the companion dog of stylish young men after the blood sport was made illegal.

training tip
Bull terriers make devoted and charming pets. However, they can be mischievous and a bit stubborn. The best way to train a bull terrier is to appeal to its fun side—otherwise the dog may become disinterested and simply walk away.

push and shove
Bull terriers are medium-sized dogs that have short, well-muscled bodies, broad chests, and muscular thighs. They are heavy dogs that are not easily pushed around. Owners of bull terriers will tell you that if anyone is going to do the shoving, it's likely to be the dog!

easy care
The bull terrier's short-haired coat is soft and flat and requires very little grooming. This breed does not drool or bark much. They have two basic needs: affection and exercise.

head geometry
There is a lot going on with the shape of the bull terrier's head, which helps set the dog apart from other breeds. The bull terrier's ears are erect and pointy, and it is the only breed that has triangular eyes.

about that egghead
Early bull terriers' heads did not have the distinctive "egghead" shape of today's dogs. This was the work of an Englishman named James Hinks, who developed the breed in the 1860s. The shape served no purpose except for looks. Maybe Hinks thought a dog that looked like its nose had been broken in a fight looked tougher!

🐾 Paws for Thought 🐾
Bullseye, the mascot for the Target department store chain, is a bull terrier.

Staffordshire Bull Terrier

Some breeds don't have the best reputations, and the Staffy is one of them. In the 1830s, when the blood sport of bullbaiting was outlawed, gamblers instead turned to dogfighting. They would pit aggressive dogs against one another and bet on which dog would win. Gamblers wanted a competitor with the agility of a terrier and the jaws of a bulldog, and the Staffordshire bull terrier was born. After dogfighting too was made illegal, aggressive traits were bred out of the Staffordshire bull terrier. Today's Staffy is a gentle, loyal family pet and a trusted companion.

do your research
In recent years, the modern Staffy has been unfairly labeled as an aggressive dog, and many end up abandoned in shelters. Owners of Staffies sometimes find they have negative social interactions with people based on fears of the breed. Some areas of the United States and Canada have bans on owning Staffordshire bull terriers because of the breed's history. The instinct to fight is buried deep in the Staffy's brain, making it essential that Staffy pups be trained and socialized to learn good dog manners. These are highly trainable and intelligent dogs, eager to please their owners, so proper training shouldn't be hard at all.

so many colors!
Staffies have short, low-maintenance coats that shed very little. They come in a variety of colors: red, fawn, white, black, blue, brindle, or any of those colors and white.

lot of dog, little package
Weighing up to 38 pounds (17 kg) but standing only 14 to 16 inches (36–41 cm) tall at the shoulder, this is a *lot* of dog stuffed into a relatively small package. A Staffy's body is rock-solid with well-defined muscles, but that doesn't stop the dog from being agile and quick.

wanna go for a walk?
Staffies require regular exercise to stay mentally and physically fit. They need a brisk daily walk but would enjoy joining their owner on a jog or a hike. These are physically fit dogs that are content to settle in for a snuggle after a good workout. If exercise needs are met, they are fine living in smaller spaces. These dogs excel at dog sports like agility, obedience, freestyle, and disc dog.

smile!

The Staffy has a large, flat head and a powerful jaw, but what really stands out is that big smile!

personality

The Staffy has a sweet nature and is a people-oriented breed. These dogs are eager to please their owners and respond well to praise. Staffies are also excellent with children, but be sure they are properly trained before leaving them unsupervised. Staffies become very attached to their owners and have often been referred to as "Velcro" dogs. They also make great therapy dogs!

🐾 Paws for Thought 🐾

The Staffy has gone by many names in the past: the Staffordshire fighting terrier, the patched fighting terrier, the bull-and-terrier, the Staffordshire pit-dog, and the brindle bull.

TOY GROUP

The dogs in the toy group have one main thing in common—they are all little dogs with big hearts (and often, big personalities). Many of these breeds have been around for centuries, immortalized in famous artworks as the lapdogs of royalty. Some are miniature versions of larger breeds, bred down to a more portable size. Most of these breeds are under 15 pounds (7 kg) and stand less than 15 inches (38 cm) tall. To be considered for the toy group, a dog must be a loving, social companion. And it doesn't hurt if they can provide a bit of amusement, too!

The Chinese crested dog is playful and loving and stands 13 inches (33 cm) at the shoulder. The breed comes in two types. One is hairless with silky tufts of hair on its head, tail, and ankles. The other is the coated variety, which is called the "powderpuff."

sporting group

hound group

working group

terrier group

toy group

non-sporting group

herding group

115

Yorkshire Terrier

One of the most popular lapdogs in the United States, Yorkies were once hardworking terriers. In the 1800s, weavers from Scotland moved to northern England to work in textile factories, bringing their terriers from different parts of Scotland with them. These terriers crossbred, creating Yorkies, which were used as ratters in mills and mines. In the late 1800s, they were recognized as a breed by the UK Kennel Club, and they instantly gained popularity as lapdogs for wealthy ladies.

grooming
The long, flowing locks of the Yorkie don't shed seasonally like the coats of many other breeds. The individual strands of hair are also finer than most dogs' coarse hair, making them more like human hair. Their coats need daily brushing if left long.

color combo
The Yorkie's floor-length coat comes in a combination of blue, gold, black, and tan.

working class to luxury living
The Yorkie's personality reflects its early days as a working terrier breed and its modern role as companion dog. These dogs are feisty but also highly affectionate with their owners.

jobs today
As well as companion dogs, Yorkies can be trained as therapy dogs. They also excel at dog sports such as rally, agility, and obedience.

🐾 Paws for Thought 🐾
Yorkshire terriers are named after Yorkshire county in England, one of the two counties where they were first developed.

Pug

Pugs were bred to do just one job, which they do exceptionally well—provide companionship for their owners. Pugs were first bred in China about 2,000 years ago to be companions to the Chinese emperor and his family. In the 1500s, Dutch traders introduced pugs to the Netherlands, where they were again adopted by royalty. Because of their loving and devoted nature, pugs quickly became popular all over Europe and eventually North America.

modern look
In the last 100 years, the pug's look has changed quite a bit. They now have shorter legs, stockier builds, bigger eyes, curly tails, and bigger eyes. All of these changes were done intentionally by mating dogs with certain characteristics.

low energy
A serious couch potato, the pug is a low-energy dog. Owners have to put in the effort to make sure pugs are exercised, especially the dogs get older.

at home in small spaces
Pugs are a top choice for city dwellers who live in apartments. They are also good pets for people who are home a lot, since pugs want to be with their owners all the time. Pugs are also quiet and don't bark much.

flatter faces
Pugs are flat-faced, like boxers and bulldogs. Because their pushed-in noses can make it difficult for them to breathe, pugs should not be exercised when it is too hot or humid outside.

expressions
With their big eyes and forehead wrinkles, pugs seem to have human-like expressions. Some scientists say humans bond more easily and closely with animals that have these expressions.

coloring
A pug's coat can be solid black, silver, or different shades of fawn with a black face mask.

🐾 Paws for Thought 🐾
A group of pugs is called a "grumble."

Chihuahua

Chihuahuas are the smallest breed of dog. Originally from Mexico, they were brought to the United States by Americans visiting the northern Mexican state of Chihuahua in the late 1800s. This is also where the breed's name comes from. No one knows exactly how Chihuahuas developed into the sassy little dogs they are today, but they likely descended from an earlier Mexican breed that is now extinct.

dangers

Owners of Chihuahuas have to make sure their pets aren't carried away by large birds of prey or by predators like coyotes. Some Chihuahuas also have a soft spot on their skulls, called a molera. Owners have to be careful that these dogs do not receive head injuries.

short legs = short walks

While Chihuahuas are high-energy dogs, their walks should be kept short because of their small size. They do not need a lot of room to run and play, and they're a good choice for people who live in apartments.

features
Chihuahuas have big features, such as erect ears and bulgy eyes, on little heads.

skull shapes
Some Chihuahuas are "apple-headed," which means their skulls are very round and there is a distinct line where the skull meets the muzzle (shown here). Others are "deer-headed." They have flatter skulls and eyes that are more widely spaced apart.

multiple personalities
Chihuahuas have different personalities. Some are nervous and jittery, while others are confident and bold. Some bark a lot, while others are very quiet.

coat
Chihuahuas come in a great variety of coat colors. Coats can be one of two types: smooth coat (shown here) or long coat.

🐾 Paws for Thought 🐾
Chihuahuas are believed to be descended from an earlier Mexican dog breed called the techichi. In the Indigenous Aztec culture, these dogs were raised and eaten for food.

Shih Tzu

Shih tzus are an ancient breed from Tibet. They were popular as palace dogs among the emperors of ancient China. Their Chinese name means "lion." It is pronounced "sheed-zoo" or "sheet-su." These dogs are believed to have been bred from two other ancient Asian breeds, the Lhasa apso and the Pekingese.

curled tail
Shih tzu tails curl up toward their backs.

lively
Shih tzus are lively little dogs that like to play. They are up to 11 inches (27 cm) tall. They are not the easiest dogs to train.

indoor dogs
Shih tzus were bred to be indoor dogs. They need short walks each day and lots of inside playtime. They are a good choice as pets for people who live in apartments.

clipping and grooming
Shih tzus that are show dogs usually have long hair. As pets, owners usually get the hair clipped because longer hair tangles easily and requires a lot of care.

cute snoot
The shih tzu has a short muzzle and an underbite.

topknot
If a shih tzu's coats is left long, the hair on the top of its head needs to be tied up in a topknot or cut so that it doesn't irritate the dog's eyes—and so it can see! The shih tzu's mustache and beard also grow to be very long.

🐾 Paws for Thought 🐾
Shih tzus have a special place in the Buddhist religion. Legends say that the Buddha himself had a shih tzu!

Pomeranian

Over the years, the feisty little Pomeranian has gotten smaller and smaller. These days, it weighs about 7 pounds (3 kg). The Pomeranian's journey to toy breed began with the spitz-type dogs of the European Arctic. In a region known as Pomerania, now part of Poland and Germany, spitzes were bred to be smaller. Favorites in Queen Victoria's kennels in England in the late 1800s, they were bred down from about 30 pounds (14 kg) to their current size.

big attitude
Pomeranians are one of the smallest dog breeds, but they have big-dog attitudes.

barking
Pomeranians are perky and alert. They can be territorial and will alert you with barking. They are also easy to train to do tricks.

hairy neck
The thicker hair around the Pomeranian's neck is referred to as its frill or mane.

coat of many colors
Pomeranians' coats come in a wider variety of colors and patterns than any other breed. They need frequent brushing.

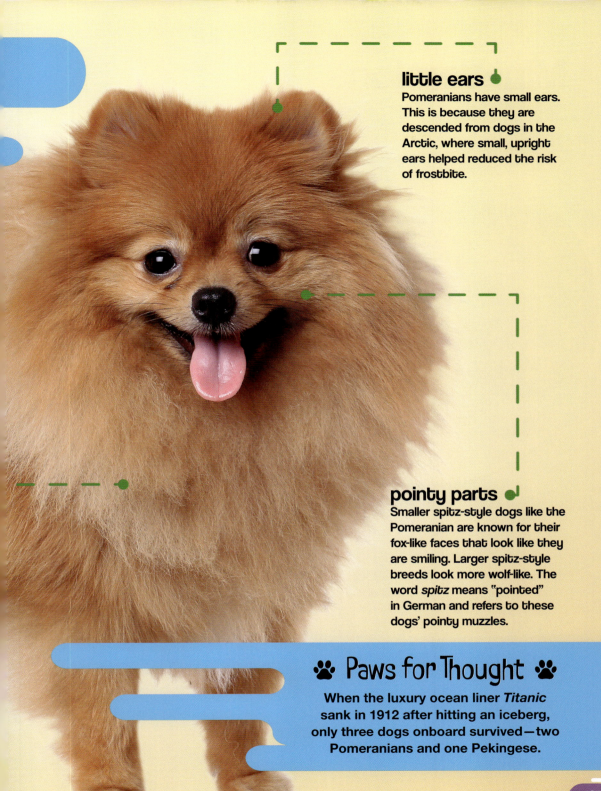

little ears
Pomeranians have small ears. This is because they are descended from dogs in the Arctic, where small, upright ears helped reduced the risk of frostbite.

pointy parts
Smaller spitz-style dogs like the Pomeranian are known for their fox-like faces that look like they are smiling. Larger spitz-style breeds look more wolf-like. The word *spitz* means "pointed" in German and refers to these dogs' pointy muzzles.

🐾 Paws for Thought 🐾
When the luxury ocean liner *Titanic* sank in 1912 after hitting an iceberg, only three dogs onboard survived—two Pomeranians and one Pekingese.

Mini-Versions

English Toy Spaniel
English toy spaniels were favorites among royalty in the 1600s. At some point in their history, they were bred with pugs to achieve their trademark flat noses and round heads. Because of their short noses, they are not tolerant of hot weather. These lovable little dogs, with their big brown eyes, were made for cuddling.

Toy Fox Terrier
The toy fox terrier is the perfect balance of relentlessly active and couch potato. Its larger cousin, the fox terrier, was bred originally for vermin control in stables and kennels. However, farmers found that the smaller dogs in the litter were very useful ratters. Soon, the toy version was developed. These fiery, clever dogs also began to find fame in circuses performing tricks!

Italian Greyhound

The Italian greyhound is very similar to its larger cousin but at a much smaller size, standing only 13 to 15 inches (33–38 cm) at the shoulder. It can reach speeds of up to 25 miles per hour (40 km/h). If you are going to own one Italian greyhound, you're better off owning two because these dogs are happier in pairs. They are very affectionate dogs and don't do well being left alone.

Toy Manchester Terrier

Named for the city in England where it was first bred, the toy Manchester terrier is easily recognized by its shiny black-and-tan coat. These nimble little terriers were bred in the mid-1800s as ratters in England's textile mills. They come in two sizes: standard and toy. The larger standard Manchester terrier belongs to the terrier group.

Toy Poodle

Some people might look at the tiny toy poodle with its poofy coat and think this dog is just for cuddles. But make no mistake—under all that fur, poodles are athletes! These little dogs can be trained for dog sports and obedience. They also love just snuggling in their favorite human's lap.

Havanese

The Havanese is the only recognized breed from Cuba. Its name comes from Havana, Cuba's capital city. Havanese were developed from bichons, which were brought to Cuba by the Spanish. They became the lapdogs of wealthy Cubans. When wealthy Cubans were forced to flee the country after the communist takeover in 1959, only a few of them managed to bring their Havanese with them to the United States, but it was enough to save the breed. It wasn't long before these outgoing, friendly little dogs became popular with Americans.

plumed tail
The tail of a Havanese is arched toward its back. Although the tail itself does not touch the dog's body, it has a long plume of tail hair that cascades over its back.

lots of hairdos
Coats come in many different colors. The outer coat is soft, silky, and wavy. The hair can be left long, clipped short by a groomer, or even corded.

sun protection
Surprisingly, their coats are not meant for warmth, but to protect them from the sun. Their silky coats are often cool to the touch.

happy walk
The front legs of a Havanese are slightly shorter than its back legs. This gives the dog the springy, bouncy walk that it's known for.

trainable
Havanese are generally very trainable. They take part in dog sports, do tricks, and can be used as therapy dogs.

🐾 Paws for Thought 🐾

The Havanese is the national dog of Cuba.

Maltese

The fashionable Maltese breed made a grand tour of the ancient world. It was a favorite breed of the ancient Greeks and Romans before being exported to China and bred with small dogs native to Asia. The newer version was then brought back to Europe looking more like the dog does today. Its name comes from the island of Malta in the Mediterranean Sea, where these dogs may have originated 2,500 years ago.

floor length
The Maltese's silky, floor-length coat can be white, lemon (off-white), or white and tan. They are also known for their high, plumed tails.

grooming
Maltese need daily brushing to prevent mats and tangles. Owners sometimes prefer to keep their hair cut short, in what is known as a "puppy cut," because it makes their coats easier to look after.

playful
Maltese have one of the longest lifespans of all dog breeds and can live for up to 15 years. They often remain playful even in their senior years.

companions
Maltese are very affectionate with their owners and are one of the oldest companion breeds. They are also good watchdogs and bark as a warning. However, they must be trained well so they don't become too barky.

button nose
Maltese are adored for their cute little button noses and large dark eyes in a sea of long white facial hair. Tears from their eyes and saliva from their mouths will stain the hair on their faces, but washing their faces regularly will help keep it white.

🐾 Paws for Thought 🐾
Bred to be constant companions, some Maltese develop separation anxiety, which means they get stressed when their owners are away from them.

Papillon

The papillon gets its name from the French word *papillon*, which means butterfly. Take one look at those ears, and it's obvious why! These tiny stunners have appeared in paintings alongside European royalty as far back as the 1600s, when they were kept as companion dogs. But don't be fooled by their small size. Papillons are a very athletic breed and excel at agility courses.

plumed tail
Ears aren't the only stunning feature on these dogs. Papillons also have long, plumed tails.

the stats
Weighing in at 5 to 10 pounds (2.3–4.5 kg) and standing at 8 to 11 inches (20–28 cm) tall, what the papi lacks in body size, it makes up for in heart.

dog with a job
Papillons thrive on mental stimulation. They are also extremely eager companions. This makes them excellent therapy dogs.

butterfly ears
Papis have large ears shaped like butterflies, which gives them their name. Some papillons have ears that lay down. Papis with these ears are known as phalenes.

brains and beauty
Papillons are extremely intelligent, eager to please, and very trainable. Papis can be trained for all types of tricks and are well-suited for competing in agility courses.

🐾 Paws for Thought 🐾
According to legend, French queen Marie Antoinette loved her papillon so much that she carried it with her on her walk to the guillotine for her beheading in 1793.

Cavalier King Charles Spaniel

Toy spaniels first rose to fame as the constant companions of England's King Charles II in the 1600s. When flatter-faced dogs from Asia, such as pugs, became popular in the 1800s, toy spaniels were bred with them to make their muzzles fashionably shorter. In the 1920s, a wealthy American offered a prize to anyone in Great Britain who could restore the toy spaniels to their old look. These old-style toy spaniels are known as Cavalier King Charles spaniels today.

Blenheim coat
King Charles spaniels have four distinct coat colors. The Blenheim coat has chestnut-colored markings on white (shown here). They can also be ruby (reddish-brown color), black and tan, or tricolor with black markings on a white background and tan on the eyes and cheeks.

coat care
King Charles spaniels have silky, wavy coats that need brushing and occasional bathing.

furry accessories
King Charles spaniels have hanging ears, plumed tails, and slippered paws.

face blaze
The white marking between the dog's eyes is called a blaze. A Blenheim King Charles also has a brown spot on the top of its head called the "Blenheim spot."

comparison
The American Kennel Club recognizes two different breeds of toy spaniels: the Cavalier King Charles spaniel and the English toy spaniel. English toy spaniels have flatter faces and are slightly smaller than the King Charles spaniel.

best of two worlds
Cavalier King Charles spaniels are one of the friendliest types of dogs. Sweet and affectionate, they will happily spend time curled up on your lap. Due to their spaniel roots, they are also lively and athletic and often compete in dog sports like agility, rally, and obedience events. With this dog, owners get the best of two worlds—an athletic dog and a toy dog all in one!

🐾 Paws for Thought 🐾
King Charles II issued a royal decree saying that toy spaniels were allowed to go anywhere. This was so he could bring his dogs wherever he went, including Parliament!

More Toy Breeds

Affenpinscher
This shaggy little dog was originally bred to catch rats in barns. Eventually, they were brought indoors to catch mice in kitchens. From there, they made their way into the hearts, and warm beds, of the owners of the house. And looking at those cute little monkey faces, who can blame them? *Affenpinscher* is German for "ape terrier."

Brussels Griffon
As the name suggests, this grumpy-looking dog was developed in Brussels, Belgium, to catch mice. The dog's wizzled mustache and beard, along with its big, dark eyes give the Griff an almost human-looking face. Griffs have larger-than-life personalities and are very eager to please when training.

Miniature Pinscher

Despite its name, the miniature pinscher, or "min pin," is not a smaller version of the Doberman pinscher. Min pins were developed to be used as ratters. They come in three colors: red, a shiny black with rust, or chocolate with rust. Min pins don't seem to realize that they stand only 13 inches (32 cm) at the shoulder, as they have the confidence and energy of much bigger dogs.

Pekingese

Pekingese are an ancient breed and were sacred in China. They were originally bred for the ancient Chinese imperial family and believed to be lions that Buddha had shrunk to miniature size. They are very strong-willed and intelligent dogs. To teach them good manners, training classes are a must.

NON-SPORTING GROUP

The dogs included in this group have nothing in common with one other except four legs and a tail! The breeds of the non-sporting group have varied job descriptions, appearances, backgrounds, and personalities. Some are extremely popular, like the French bulldog, while others, such as the schipperke, are less common. Some of the dogs in this group may have originally been bred as working dogs, but over the years they've become companion animals.

sporting group

hound group

working group

terrier group

toy group

non-sporting group

herding group

The schipperke's name (pronounced "skip-er-kee"), means "little captain" in Flemish. They were originally bred for catching rats. These little dogs, which stand only 13 inches (33 cm) at the shoulder, were also used as watchdogs. Their fluffy coats hide powerful jaws and muscular bodies.

French Bulldog

The Frenchie is the most popular dog breed in the United States according to the American Kennel Club. This breed got its start when English lacemakers brought their miniature bulldogs to France. There, the dogs were bred with pugs and terriers to create the French bulldog. Known as excellent companions for city dwellers, their popularity spread rapidly.

body
Frenchies are small dogs with sturdy, compact bodies. Their coats can be a solid color, such as black, fawn, Isabella (fawn with a blue-gray tinge), or lilac (a brownish-blue with a purple tinge). Coats can also have patterns such as brindle or merle.

easy on the treats
French bulldogs are not an active breed and are content to take short daily walks. However, they're playful whether indoors or outside. These dogs are prone to gaining too much weight, so treats must be kept to a minimum—if you can resist that cute face.

bat ears
The Frenchie's large, rounded ears are one of its most distinctive features.

flat and square
French bulldogs have large, square heads. Their short muzzles make them one of the flat-faced breeds.

friendly and quiet
French bulldogs are generally friendly with people and with other dogs. They do not bark much.

🐾 Paws for Thought 🐾
In 2022, Frenchies became America's most popular dog. They took the top spot from the Labrador retriever, which had been the favorite for 31 years!

Boston Terrier

The Boston terrier is the perfect example of what can sometimes go wrong—or very right—when breeders try to mate two breeds to get desired traits. The Boston was originally intended to be an athletic blood sport fighter, created by crossbreeding a bulldog with an English white terrier. Instead, what breeders got was an incredibly sweet, polite dog. Bostons quickly became popular in the city of Boston, which is how they got their name.

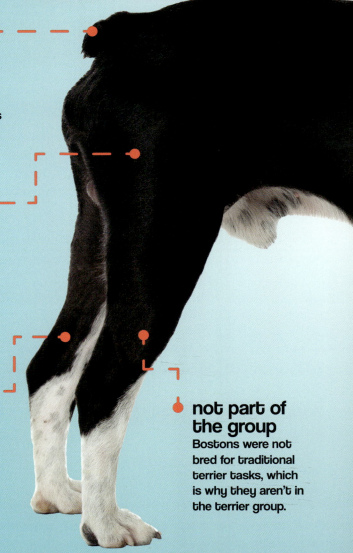

stubby tail
Bostons have short tails that can be straight, crooked, or curled up tight against their bodies. Some Bostons have tails that are just tiny little nubs.

comparison
Boston terriers are sometimes confused with French bulldogs, especially Frenchies whose coats are brindle and white or black and white. Bostons have rounder heads, pointier ears, and leaner bodies than Frenchies.

cuddle monster
Bostons are sweet, cuddly, and like to be within touching—or staring—distance of their owners. When you get home, they will be super excited to see you—and anyone else who comes to the door.

not part of the group
Bostons were not bred for traditional terrier tasks, which is why they aren't in the terrier group.

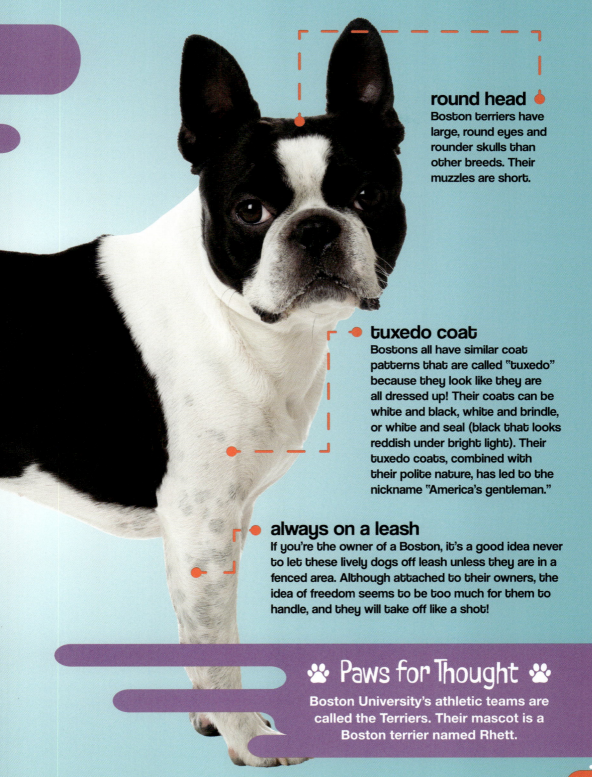

round head
Boston terriers have large, round eyes and rounder skulls than other breeds. Their muzzles are short.

tuxedo coat
Bostons all have similar coat patterns that are called "tuxedo" because they look like they are all dressed up! Their coats can be white and black, white and brindle, or white and seal (black that looks reddish under bright light). Their tuxedo coats, combined with their polite nature, has led to the nickname "America's gentleman."

always on a leash
If you're the owner of a Boston, it's a good idea never to let these lively dogs off leash unless they are in a fenced area. Although attached to their owners, the idea of freedom seems to be too much for them to handle, and they will take off like a shot!

🐾 Paws for Thought 🐾
Boston University's athletic teams are called the Terriers. Their mascot is a Boston terrier named Rhett.

Bulldog

Also known as English bulldogs, the "bull" in their name comes from their early role as dogs used in bullbaiting. In England in the Middle Ages, bullbaiting was a gruesome blood sport in which packs of dogs would be pitted against bulls in a fight to the death while spectators bet on the outcome. When bullbaiting was outlawed in 1835, bulldogs found themselves without a job. Over time, they were bred to be smaller and less aggressive, though their past image as brawlers makes them a popular mascot for many sports teams.

keep calm and carry on
Today's bulldogs are calm and friendly, and they're good pets for families with children. Though easygoing, they are not lazy and need the proper amount of exercise to ensure they don't become overweight.

wide and stocky
Bulldogs are built low to the ground and have sturdy legs that support their stocky bodies and wide chests. The dog's head is large compared to the rest of the body.

granddaddy
The bulldog is the granddaddy of many other dog breeds, including bull-type terriers, the French bulldog, and the Boston terrier.

sourmug
The wrinkles and folds of a bulldog's face make it look like it is grumpy. They are sometimes nicknamed "sourmugs."

wrinkly for a reason
Bulldogs' distinct facial features were important during their bullbaiting days. Their large, undershot jaws meant a vice-like grip. Their face wrinkles trapped blood to keep it out of their eyes and noses. Their flat noses allowed them to breathe if they were hanging on to a bull by their teeth.

🐾 Paws for Thought 🐾
British prime minister Winston Churchill was given the nickname the "British Bulldog" due to his face jowls and his fighting spirit during World War II (1939–1945). Churchill had a bulldog named Dodo and poodle named Rufus.

Bichon Frise

The bichon frise (pronounced "bee-shawn free-zay") is often described as charming and peppy. At one time popular as the pampered pets of European nobles, these dogs are also known for their role as performers in circuses. Bichons frises crave being the center of attention and are easy to train to do tricks. In fact, teaching them new tricks helps them from becoming too overbearing.

little white dogs
A bichon's trademark is its velvety, plush, pure-white coat, but some dogs may have cream or apricot-colored markings.

get thee to a groomer!
Bichons frises are high-maintenance when it comes to their coats. Hair can shed from their coats and get trapped in their dense undercoats, so they have to be brushed out daily to avoid tangles and mats. They need frequent baths and trips to the groomer to keep that "bichon look."

city living
Bichons frises are small dogs that grow to about 12 inches (29 cm) to the shoulder and weigh less than 18 pounds (8 kg). They make great pets for city dwellers and are surprisingly fast runners when allowed to run freely at off-leash dog parks.

poofs
Bichons' wavy hair gives them a poofy look. They always have large, dark eyes and little button noses.

look at me!
These dogs love to be in the spotlight and will often do tricks or put on a show to get attention. They generally get along well with other dogs and children.

🐾 Paws for Thought 🐾
Bichons frises often appeared in European paintings.

Lhasa Apso

This little dog's history is the only thing longer than its hair. Lhasa apsos have existed since the 800s. They were watchdogs in Tibetan **Buddhist** monasteries in the Himalayan mountain range of Tibet. They also guarded the inside of temples and palaces, while huge Tibetan mastiffs guarded the outside. Lhasas were considered sacred and were associated with guardian snow lions from Tibetan folklore. Lhasa apsos were rarely ever sold. Instead they were given as gifts as a symbol of good fortune.

body
A Lhasa's tail curls over its back, like all Tibetan breeds' tails do. They stand 11 inches (28 cm) at the shoulder and weigh up to 18 pounds (8 kg).

all about hair
When fully grown out, Lhasa apsos have lovely floor-length, flat coats that part in the middle. Whether the hair is kept long or short, Lhasas will still have to be groomed and clipped regularly.

exercise
Lhasas are pros at exercising themselves. They will race around their homes or yards to burn off energy—the "zoomies" in dog-lover lingo. But that doesn't mean they won't enjoy a walk with their favorite human!

watchdog
These dogs were bred to be patient, courageous, and independent. They form strong bonds with their owners and make excellent watchdogs.

big attitude
Lhasas can be strong-willed. Training is a must so they can learn good manners.

the right job
Lhasa apsos make great therapy dogs. They have an attentive nature and a love of people.

🐾 Paws for Thought 🐾

The Lhasa apso is one of three Tibetan breeds in the non-sporting group. The other two are the Tibetan terrier and the Tibetan spaniel.

Poodle

Forget everything you think you know about poodles from cartoons and TV shows. Poodles are athletic and extremely intelligent. They originated in Germany as duck-hunting retrievers but have been bred into three sizes: standard, miniature, and toy. No matter the size, they all share the same characteristics.

poodle clip
Poodles are usually groomed in one of two styles. The continental clip has puffs of hair, called pompons, left around the dog's ankles, leg joints, tail tip, head, and chest. The sporting clip is a close shave that follows the shape of the dog.

swimmers
Because poodles were first used to retrieve ducks, they are good swimmers. Hunters originally created the continental clip grooming style to keep the dogs' sensitive parts warm in cold water, and they shaved the rest to make them faster swimmers.

daily brushing
A poodle's tight-knit curls help the dog stay warm in cold weather. Their coats are non-shedding, but they need to be brushed daily because mats can form at the roots.

at work
In addition to retrieving ducks, poodles have been trained to be truffle hunters and circus performers.

small, medium, or large
Miniature poodles are the mid-sized version of the poodle. They are up to 15 inches (38 cm) high at the shoulder. Standard poodles are anything taller than this, and toy poodles are 10 inches (25 cm) high or less.

natural athlete
Poodles of any size are high-energy dogs. They need be exercised frequently. They are good dogs to take on runs or swims, and they enjoy games like fetch. Poodles are often champions in dog sport competitions.

🐾 Paws for Thought 🐾
Standard poodles were bred down to the miniature version in France. Toy poodles were bred to be even smaller in the United States.

Dalmatian

Dalmatians are known for their spots and as mascots at fire stations. One of their first jobs was as "coach dogs." Coach dogs ran alongside horse-drawn stagecoaches to protect the horses from attacks from other dogs, and the people inside from robbers. Before firetrucks were invented, firefighters arrived at fires by coach. Dalmatians ran ahead of the fire-coach to clear away crowds so the firefighters could get through the streets to the fire.

spotty
A dalmatian's spots are as unique as a human's fingerprints or a tiger's stripes—no two are exactly the same! Underneath their coats, their skin is also spotted. Dalmatians can have either black or liver (brown) spots.

runners
Dalmatians have great endurance and can run long distances. They are spot-on for people who like running or jogging with their pet.

daily activity
Dalmatians are an active breed, so they need plenty of exercise. Without proper activity, they can become destructive or try to escape.

protective
Originally bred to guard horses and coaches, dalmatians' territorial instinct makes them loyal watchdogs.

athletic
A dalmatian's body is sleek and muscular. These athletic dogs perform well in dog sports such as agility, tracking, and lure coursing.

size
Dalmatians are medium-sized dogs. They grow up to 24 inches (61 cm) tall and weigh up to 70 pounds (32 kg).

🐾 Paws for Thought 🐾
Dalmatians are born without spots. Puppies begin to get spots when they are around two weeks old. The spots continue to develop for about a year.

Shiba Inu

The Shiba Inu is one of six original Japanese dog breeds. Shiba Inus were bred for flushing out birds and small game for hunters in the mountains of Japan. They are known as alert, bold, and energetic dogs. They are the most popular breed in Japan, and they've become famous worldwide for their quirky behavior and antics.

cute curls
The high, curly tail of the Shiba Inu is not just cute to look at. It's curled to keep it close to the body to preserve body heat. There are three tail types: a single curl, a double curl, and a sickle tail, which is a half curl that points toward the dog's back.

coat
Shiba Inus shed a lot! They have thick double coats that help them stay warm. The coat can be red, cream, sesame (red hair tipped with black), or black and tan.

build
The Shiba Inu is the smallest of the Japanese breeds, and it has a sturdy, muscular build.

fox-like
With its triangle-shaped face and pointy ears, the Shiba Inu looks kind of like a fox.

screams and yodels
Shiba Inus have scream-like barks. They also make a sound like a yodel when excited, and sometimes they even purr like a cat when being pet!

markings
The white markings on and around a Shiba Inu's face are called *urajiro*, which is a Japanese word meaning "white underside." Only the white markings on the face, neck, chest, and stomach are called *urajiro*.

🐾 Paws for Thought 🐾
Shiba Inus are known for their loyalty. During an earthquake in Japan in 2004, a Shiba Inu named Mari saved her owner, who was trapped under a cupboard.

Xoloitzcuintli

Xoloitzcuintli is a dog breed from Mexico. Its name comes from the dog-headed Aztec god Xolotl, combined with the word *itzcuintli*, which means "dog" in Nahuatl, the language of the Aztecs. Xoloitzcuintli is pronounced "show-low-uht-skwint-lee." These dogs are known for their very short hair or for being hairless. They are considered a national treasure in Mexico.

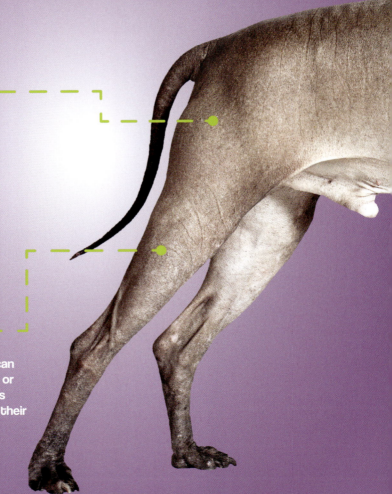

sleek and shiny
Xolos have thick, sleek skin. Hairless types produce an oil on their skin that helps protect them from the sun and insects and gives them a rich shine. Their skin does have to be cleaned occasionally to remove dead skin cells, which can cause acne.

size and coat
Xolos come in three sizes: toy, miniature, and standard. They can be bred to have very short hair or to be hairless. The hairless dogs still have some coarse hairs on their heads, tails, and feet.

activity
Xolos are described as calm and dignified. Though lean and muscular, they are not extremely active.

personality
Xolos are intelligent, even-tempered, affectionate, and playful.

space heaters
Due to their lack of hair, Xolos give off a lot of body heat. People who have them as pets often enjoy cuddling them because they are so warm.

hypoallergenic
The Xolo may be a good choice as a pet for people who have allergies to dog hair.

🐾 Paws for Thought 🐾

The Aztec people of Mexico believed that Xolos had healing powers and that they accompanied the souls of the dead through the afterlife.

Chinese Shar-Pei

The Chinese shar-pei was bred in China at least 2,000 years ago. A multipurpose dog, the breed was used to guard royal palaces, for hunting, and to herd and protect livestock. Although once popular as watchdogs, by 1978 they were declared the world's rarest breed. International dog organizations stepped in to help save the breed, and after appearing on the cover of *Time* magazine in 1979, their popularity skyrocketed in the United States.

wrinkly body armor
Not the most ferocious or agile fighter, the shar-pei's natural advantage in a fight is its loose, wrinkly skin. When another dog bites a shar-pei, it gets a mouthful of skin rather than puncturing the shar-pei's skin and harming its internal organs.

coat
The shar-pei's Chinese name means "rough, sandy coat" in English. Its hair is short, coarse, and feels a bit like sandpaper. Their coats can be apricot, black, brown, blue (silver), fawn, chocolate, or cream colored.

exercise
Compared to some other breeds, such as retrievers, shar-peis do not require a lot of exercise. They aren't much for swimming either.

personality
The shar-pei has a strong guarding instinct and can be aloof with people it doesn't know. But generally they are very laid-back.

small ears
During fights, small ears meant extra protection for the shar-pei. With smaller ears, there was less for another animal to grab on to.

hippo mouth
With its broad, hippopotamus-looking muzzle, this dog was bred to look fierce.

🐾 Paws for Thought 🐾
The shar-pei and the chow chow are the only two dog breeds with blue tongues.

More Non-Sporting Dogs

Finnish Spitz
Like the Shiba Inu, the Finnish spitz looks something like a fox. This dog has been given the nickname "Barking Bird Dog" because it will yodel continuously to alert a hunter to the location of game birds. In Finland, where these dogs originated, they even participate in barking competitions!

Chow Chow
Like the shar-pei, the chow chow originated in ancient China. It also has a blue tongue. The chow chow has a dense double coat with extra-thick hair around its neck, giving the dog the appearance of having a mane like a lion!

Löwchen

The löwchen's name is German for "little lion." Traditionally they were groomed in a style known as a "lion clip" (shown here). These lively little dogs are eager to please their owners and are popular pets in Europe.

American Eskimo Dog

American Eskimo dogs, or "Eskies" for short, come in three sizes: standard, miniature, and toy. These beautiful dogs have brilliant white coats with lion-like ruffs around the chest.

HERDING GROUP

As their name suggests, dogs in the herding group were bred for herding livestock, including sheep, cattle, and even reindeer! Breeds in the herding group are some of the top dogs when it comes to intelligence and athleticism. Their jobs as herders meant they needed a high level of energy. As pets, herding dogs need to get plenty of exercise and have jobs to do, otherwise they may start herding family members! However, this natural drive to keep busy also makes them highly trainable.

sporting group

hound group

working group

terrier group

toy group

non-sporting group

herding group

The Icelandic sheepdog is the only breed that originated in Iceland, where the dog was used to herd sheep and ponies.

German Shepherd

Known for their loyalty, courage, and confidence, German shepherds are one of the top three most popular dogs in the United States. They are fearless in their willingness to put their own lives on the line for others, making them excellent guardians. Easy to train to respond to different commands, German shepherds are valued as large, gentle family pets as well as trusted working dogs.

coat
The large patch of black hair on the German shepherd's back is known as a saddle because of its shape. The dog's thick double coat is usually black and tan or red and black. These dogs shed a lot and need regular brushing.

body shape
German shepherds are built strong, with long bodies and bushy tails. Some dogs have sloped backs, while others have flat backs. Male dogs are usually about 26 inches (66 cm) from the ground to the shoulder and weigh up to 90 pounds (41 kg). Females are slightly smaller than males.

what's up, ears?
German shepherd puppies are born with floppy ears. Their ears start to stand up when they are anywhere from eight weeks to six months old.

super smart
German shepherds are quick learners and eager to please. They are healthiest when they have tasks to do, which can include jobs or dog sports such as dock diving, flyball, tracking, and agility.

at work
Because of their intelligence, trainability, and fearlessness, German shepherds do a number of jobs. They are used in police work, as military dogs, as guide and service dogs, for search-and-rescue, and as guard dogs.

🐾 Paws for Thought 🐾
Two German shepherds have their own stars on the Hollywood Walk of Fame. The dogs' names were Strongheart and Rin Tin Tin, and they appeared in many films.

Pembroke Welsh Corgi

Don't confuse the Pembroke Welsh corgi for a cute little toy dog. These dogs were made for herding. Their stubby little legs worked to their advantage when herding cattle because being low to the ground meant they could nip at livestock's heels to get them to move without being kicked. Corgis are still used on farms as herders, but they have recently become one of the most popular pet breeds.

tail or no tail
Pembroke Welsh corgis usually have very short or no tails. Another type of corgi, the Cardigan Welsh corgi, looks very similar to the Pembroke but has a longer tail that is sometimes big and bushy like a fox's tail.

activity
Corgis are athletic and need space and time to run. They often compete in dog sports such as herding and agility events. They respond well to attention from their owners, which makes them ready and willing for training.

short legs
A corgi looks like it has a big dog's body on a small dog's legs. But its little legs and thick thighs have a lot of power, making them faster and more agile runners than they may seem.

personality
Corgis are little dogs with big-dog personalities. They can be fearless, independent, and good watchdogs.

bossy barkers
Corgis were bred to be bossy, and along with that comes their bark. Their barking does make them good watchdogs, but too much barking at nothing can be a sign a corgi is not receiving enough stimulation.

🐾 Paws for Thought 🐾
Corgis were a favorite pet of Great Britain's Queen Elizabeth II. She owned more than 30 of them in her lifetime.

Collie

Collies were originally bred in Scotland to herd sheep, and like many herding breeds, they are known for their agility and stamina. Collies made the leap from farmhand to pet in the 1860s when Great Britain's Queen Victoria discovered the breed and adopted some as part of her "Royal Kennel." Collies quickly became a favorite choice among the queen's followers. Said to be gentle and caring, today they are popular family pets.

size
Under all that fur, collies are medium-sized, narrow dogs. They are usually between 22 to 26 inches (56–66 cm) tall from the ground to their shoulders and weigh between 50 and 75 pounds (23–34 kg).

gorgeous coat
Collies can be either smooth-coated or rough. Rough collies have longer, denser fur. They require lots of brushing to avoid matted, tangled hair. A collie's coat can be any combination of sable (an earthy brown color) and white, tricolor, blue merle (black and gray), or white.

faces
Collies have wedge-shaped heads, expressive eyes, and long pointy snoots.

play, rest, repeat
Collies like to play and go on long walks to burn off their energy. Dogs that get enough exercise are content to chill around the house with their families.

happy helpers
Collies are quick to learn and eager to please, which makes them good companions and therapy dogs. As pets, they must be properly trained when young.

🐾 Paws for Thought 🐾

A 1950s TV show called *Lassie* made collies popular in the United States. In the show, Lassie was always helping rescue her owner, a boy named Timmy.

Australian Shepherd

Although you might think that the Australian shepherd comes from Australia, it is actually a breed from California. It is a cross between European sheepdogs and collies used as herding dogs in Australia. Australian shepherds are known for their work as ranch hands, herding sheep and cattle. There is no limit to what an Australian shepherd will herd—they can sometimes be found at rodeos herding bulls!

straight or wavy

Australian shepherds have a variety of looks. Some have straight hair, while others have wavy hair. Their coats have an irregular pattern known as merle or dapple. Their coats can be blue (gray) merle, red merle, red, and black. These dogs are heavy shedders and need frequent brushing.

tale of two tails

Australian shepherds can be born with a naturally bobbed tail or a long tail. Ranchers sometimes purposely breed Australian shepherds with naturally short tails because they think it's safer for the dog when it is herding.

brown, blue, or both?
Australian shepherds can have brown or blue eyes. And sometimes they have one of each!

shy
Australian shepherds are intelligent and form close bonds with family members, often following them around. They can be shy with new people and take a while to warm up to them.

many jobs
Because they are so smart, Australian shepherds are suited to many different jobs, such as rodeo performers, therapy dogs, drug detectors, guide dogs for the blind, and search-and-rescue dogs. Australian shepherds don't tire easily and have the physical stamina to work long days.

🐾 Paws for Thought 🐾
Australian shepherds have had many different names: Spanish shepherds, bob-tails, California shepherds, and pastor dogs.

Border Collie

Possibly the smartest and most hardworking dog there is, the border collie is known for its agility, trainability, and high energy level. Because of their intense drive to do work, these dogs are best suited for experienced dog owners and as working dogs. They were originally bred in the area around the boundary between Scotland and northern England, which is where the word *border* in their name comes from.

dog sports
Border collies are athletic, medium-sized dogs that are slightly smaller than collies. They excel at flyball and agility competitions.

speed and grace
Border collies aren't the fastest breed, but they are one of the fastest herding dogs. They can run at a top speed of 30 miles per hour (48 km/h). Only a few breeds in the hound and sporting groups are faster.

look into my eyes
When herding, border collies get in front of sheep and give them an intense stare to intimidate them.

many-colored coats
Border collies come in a variety of colors and patterns. The American Kennel Club recognizes 17 different coat colors for border collies.

🐾 Paws for Thought 🐾
Chaser the border collie is thought to be the world's smartest dog. Chaser was able to learn the meanings of more than 1,000 different words!

Australian Cattle Dog

Unlike Australian shepherds, Australian cattle dogs did originally come from Australia, where they were bred from wild dingoes. Australian cattle dogs are also called blue heelers, which comes from the color of their coats and the way they nip at the heels of cattle to get them moving when herding. Like many other breeds in the herding group, Australian cattle dogs thrive when doing some kind of work or activity with their owners.

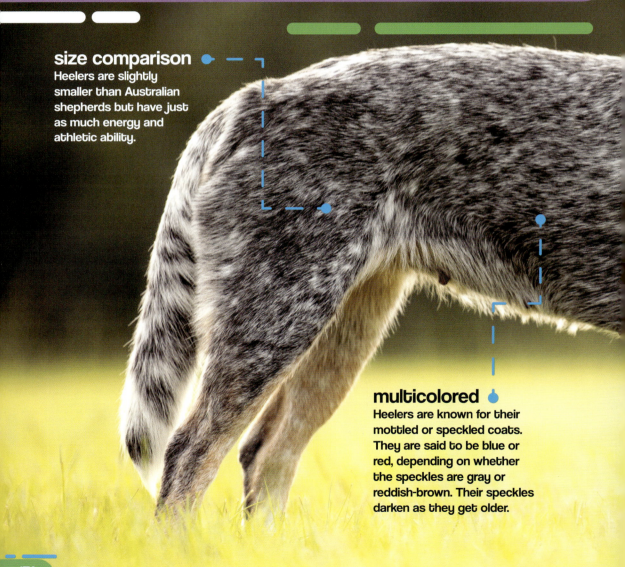

size comparison
Heelers are slightly smaller than Australian shepherds but have just as much energy and athletic ability.

multicolored
Heelers are known for their mottled or speckled coats. They are said to be blue or red, depending on whether the speckles are gray or reddish-brown. Their speckles darken as they get older.

outdoor living
Blue heelers are suited for being outdoors and are best for homes that have a lot of room to exercise, such as in the countryside. If they live in cities, they will need to be socialized with other dogs and people from an early age and taken out for exercise often.

active body, active mind
Australian cattle dogs need to keep their minds active as well as their bodies. In addition to herding, they excel at dog sports such as agility and flyball. At home, owners will need to have a variety of dog puzzles, chews, and tug toys when heelers are indoors to keep them occupied.

🐾 Paws for Thought 🐾
The animated children's show *Bluey* is about the adventures of a family of Australian cattle dogs.

Belgian Malinois

The Belgian Malinois is sometimes called the "Superman of dogs" because of the amazing physical feats it can be trained to do. These dogs can scale tall vertical walls and make long jumps where they seem to fly through the air. Malinois were first bred in city of Maline, in the country of Belgium, for herding and guarding. Today, these fearless athletes can be found working anywhere there is danger. No task or sport is too extreme for this breed.

loyalty
Belgian Malinois form intense bonds with their handlers, which makes them obedient for police work and security jobs. These dogs are also elite super soldiers, trained as combat assault dogs to work alongside the military's Navy SEALs.

brains and brawn
Malinois have strong personalities, extreme focus, and devotion to work and learning. Their owners must be willing to train and work with them every day so they do not become bored.

face masks
Malinois' coats range from a light fawn to a dark mahogany color. They all have black markings around their eyes and mouths, which makes them look kind of like they are wearing superhero masks!

comparison
Both Belgian Malinois and German shepherds are used in police work. While both dog breeds are powerful and agile, Belgian Malinois are smaller, lighter, and more compact than German shepherds. They also have less hair than German shepherds.

jumpers and climbers
With their lean, tight bodies and well-muscled legs, Malinois can jump clean over a person who is 6 feet (1.8 m) tall! They think nothing of propelling themselves over walls, fences, and even up trees!

🐾 Paws for Thought 🐾
Belgian Malinois have been trained by the military to skydive!

Bouvier des Flandres

The Bouvier des Flandres was originally bred as a cattle herder. But farmers in France, where this breed is from, were looking for a dog that could do everything from keep watch to pull carts. Over time, these dogs became valuable not only as herders but also for tasks that required strength. They are so successful as multitaskers that Bouviers were even used by the Belgian army during World War I (1914–1918).

coat
The Bouvier's waterproof double coat needs a good brushing once a week. The coat color can be fawn, black, gray brindle, or "salt and pepper."

big bones, big dog
Bouviers have heavy bones and powerful muscles and can weigh as much as 110 pounds (50 kg). Up to 28 inches (71 cm) tall from ground to shoulder, they are one of the largest, sturdiest dogs in the herding group.

watchdog
Bouviers are intelligent, even-tempered, and independent. They make great watchdogs.

facial hair
The Bouvier's mustache and beard help protect its face by catching dirt and debris. If kept as pets, they need a good face washing every once in a while.

square-shaped
With its long sturdy legs and short, broad back, the Bouvier is said to have a perfect square proportion. This shape makes the breed ideal for pulling heavy carts.

🐾 Paws for Thought 🐾
Due to the devastation that two world wars caused in Belgium, Bouviers nearly became extinct. Thankfully, small numbers of them were kept alive in other countries.

Old English Sheepdog

Despite its name, the old English sheepdog isn't a sheepdog. It's not one of the oldest breeds, either! These dogs were bred in western England just a few hundred years ago. Back then, they were used for driving cattle to market. Today, these shaggy dogs are popular as pets due to their goofy, kind, and protective nature.

bodies
Old English sheepdogs have large rumps (behinds) and compact, muscular bodies.

loads of hair
The old English sheepdog's coat does an excellent job of keeping the dog warm and dry in cold, wet weather.

large paws
Sheepdogs shuffle when they walk but are quite nimble when they need to be.

hidden eyes
Even though their facial hair is long, sheepdogs can still see through it. They usually have brown or blue eyes, and sometimes one of each!

boom!
Sheepdogs have loud, booming barks that have been described as sounding like pots being banging together.

🐾 Paws for Thought 🐾
At one time, these dogs were shorn like sheep each year, and their hair was spun into yarn!

Puli

A puli's most recognizable feature is—you guessed it!—its hair. Pulis are believed to have developed their unique coat more than 1,000 years ago, when they were introduced to the harsh climate of the plains of eastern Hungary. Without trees, these dogs were unprotected from the wind, rain, and cold while working as sheepdogs. Over time, their long hair naturally matted together to form cords, which these dogs are still known for today.

head or tail?

With its high tail and entire body covered in hair, it can be hard to tell which end is the front of the dog and which is the rear.

coat

The puli's outercoat starts to clump together to form cords when the dog is six to nine months old. It takes several years of growth before the full coat is corded. A puli's hair can be gray, black, or white.

intelligent
Pulis are intelligent and friendly. They are usually obedient and do well at agility events.

family flock
As pets, pulis are dedicated family members and will try to guard people as they would a flock of sheep—they might even try herding them!

body
Pulis are medium-sized dogs that grow to be about 17 inches (43 cm) tall. Though they may look heavy, they only weigh about 35 pounds (16 kg). One-fifth of that weight is its cords.

🐾 Paws for Thought 🐾

A puli named Beast is probably the original social media influencer. His human is Mark Zuckerberg, founder of Facebook. Beast has more than 2.4 million Facebook followers!

More Herders

Finnish Lapphund
These dogs were bred for herding one animal in particular—reindeer! Originally from Lapland, an area north of the Arctic Circle, these small herders are quick and agile to avoid getting hit by reindeer antlers.

Canaan Dog
The Canaan dog is the national dog of Israel. A very old breed of desert dog, it has been used for many different jobs over the years because it is energetic, smart, and trainable.

Briard
Briards come from France, where they were bred to herd and protect large flocks of sheep. They are known for their luxurious beards and eyebrows.

Mudi
Mudis are rare sheep-herding dogs from Hungary. They are mainly used today as rescue dogs in Finland.

Pumi
The pumi is a small, compact sheep-herding dog originally from Hungary. Their small size allowed them to easily move their flocks through narrow roads connecting pastures.

Swedish Vallhund
Similar to corgis, Swedish vallhunds were bred to be long and low to the ground so they could nip at cattle without getting kicked. This breed dates back 1,200 years.

Shetland Sheepdog
Shelties are miniature versions of collies that come from Scotland. They were bred to move sheep, ponies, and poultry.

MIXED BREEDS

A mixed breed, or hybrid dog, is the offspring of two different purebred dog breeds. Breeders often choose dogs that have specific traits in the hopes that the offspring will have the desirable traits. Some hybrid dogs become very popular as pets. Poodles are common for mixed breeds because of their hypoallergenic quality and non-shedding coats.

Goldendoodle
Golden Retriever & Poodle

Labradoodle
Labrador Retriever & Poodle

Borador
Border Collie & Labrador

Puggle
Pug & Beagle

Pomsky
Pomeranian & Siberian Husky

Cockapoo
Cocker Spaniel & Poodle

Bernedoodle
Bernese Mountain Dog & Poodle

Chiweenie
Chihuahua & Dachshund

Cavapoo
Cavalier King Charles Spaniel & Poodle

Yorkipoo
Yorkshire Terrier & Poodle

ADOPTING

Purebred dogs can be purchased from breeders. Many breeders are registered with kennel clubs and belong to breed clubs. Registered breeders follow a code of ethics to ensure that they are breeding dogs responsibly. They choose dogs for mating to ensure that puppies will be healthy and meet breed standards. Good breeders interview potential dog owners to make sure that they will be suitable owners for that breed. There are often waiting lists for puppies that come from breeders.

Rescues

Rescue organizations are another place to get a purebred dog. Some rescue organizations focus on a specific breed. The dogs available for adoption from rescue organizations may have been abandoned or mistreated by their previous owners. Adopting a dog from a rescue organization may be a better option for people who have previous experience with dogs, as these dogs' history is unknown. Sometimes dogs are surrendered to rescue organizations by their owners if they cannot care for the dog properly. These are usually older dogs rather than puppies.

Shelters

People who cannot care for their dogs any longer often leave them at animal shelters. This is usually the fault of the owner rather than the fault of the dog. People who get dogs may not realize the amount of time, effort, and money it takes to care for a dog. Or they may be moving and cannot take the dog with them. Other dogs at shelters are strays or lost dogs. Some of the dogs found at shelters are purebred dogs, but most are mixed breeds. At a shelter, dogs are cared for until someone adopts them. Sadly, shelters can become overcrowded and dogs that have been there for too long are euthanized if no one wants to adopt them. Adopting a dog from a shelter can mean saving a dog's life.

Adopting

Adopting a dog from a rescue or a shelter instead of buying one from a breeder can be a very rewarding experience. But adoption also means getting a dog whose history is unknown. The dog may not have been trained properly by its previous owner, or it may have been mistreated. These dogs will need extra time and attention to train. Other shelter or rescue dogs may be very well trained. People who adopt dogs from shelters can find out what breeds their dogs are made up of by getting a DNA test done. Some of the best pets are mixed breeds from shelters or rescues. After all, the characteristics of a breed only go so far in determining what a dog will be like. The dog's personality and the quality of training they receive play a large part in shaping the dog.

GLOSSARY

adapted Made suitable for a different use over time

adversaries Opponents in a fight or contest

aerodynamic A shape that allows something to move easily through the air

afterlife A belief in a life after death

aggression Attack behaviors, such as snarling, growling, lunging, and biting

agility The ability of the body to change direction quickly and smoothly

ancestor The animal one is descended from

anxiety A feeling of extreme worry or unease

arson The intentional setting of a fire, causing damage

assertive Having a lot of confidence and not easily intimidated

athleticism Physical qualities that make one good at sports

baritone A medium-deep sound

blood sport A sport involving much bloodshed

bobbed Short

breeding Controlled mating to produce desired offspring

brindle A coat pattern that is striped

Buddhist Relating to Buddhism, a faith based on the teaching of the Buddha

canine An animal belonging to the Canidae animal family

characteristics Qualities that make something unique

co-existed Having lived together at the same time

communist Describing a political system in which all goods are owned and controlled by the state

corded A rope-like dog coat in which hairs of the topcoat and undercoat are twisted together

disabilities Conditions that make it difficult for people to do what others can

disc dog A dog sport event in which dogs catch a disc

disposition One's usual mood or attitude

DNA test A test to determine a dog's breed background

double coat A dog's coat made up of two separate layers of hair

driving A type of herding in which livestock is forced to move forward

ecosystem The community of living things in an area

elongated Something that is very long

endurance The ability to do something for a long period of time

even-tempered Not easily angered or annoyed

evolved Changed over time

extinct No longer in existence

fowl Any kind of bird

grooming Cleaning and maintaining an animal, especially its coat

ground cover The small plants that cover the ground

guard dog A dog that provides protection

guide dogs Dogs specially trained to help people with vision problems

hindquarters The back half of a four-legged animal

immigrants People who have moved to a new country

immortalized Describing something that continues to live on after it passes

Indigenous people The first people to live in a place

infestation An attack or invasion of something unwanted, usually insects or other pests

instinct A natural behavior one is born with

insulated Something that has been lined or covered to prevent energy loss

internal organs Soft, inside body parts needed for the body to do certain functions, such as the heart or liver

invasive species Plants or animals introduced to an area and causing harm to the natural environment

jowls The fleshy lower parts of the cheeks

liver A dark-brown color in the coats of dogs and horses

livestock Farm animals kept for doing work or to make products such as meat or wool

lure coursing A dog sport for sight hounds in which they follow a small moving object that mimics prey

matted Hair tangled into a knot

mature To become an adult

Middle Ages A period of European history from about 500 to 1500 CE

molecules Very small units of something

multitaskers Dogs or people that can perform many different tasks or jobs

nasal cavities Spaces inside the nose where receptor cells that detect odor molecules are found

nerves Clusters of cells inside the body that send signals that allow movement

nobility A high-ranking social class

obedience Voluntary behaviors a dog does on cue, such as sitting

overbearing Something dominating or controlling

paw pads The layer of specialized skin and fat on the bottom of dogs' feet

peasant A farmer who did not own the land they worked in the Middle Ages

plumed Hair that is full and carried high

prey drive An animal's natural instinct to find, chase, and capture prey

prohibited Not allowed by law

purebred Having parents from the same breed

registry An official record of things

repellent Something that drives something else away

reprimands Scoldings or criticisms

resilient Able to bounce back or recover quickly

scent receptors Proteins that bind odor molecules to olfactory cells

seizure A period of unusual activity in the brain that causes involuntary movements

smuggled Brought somewhere illegally

socialization Preparing a dog for positive interactions with other dogs

species A group of similar organisms able to reproduce

stamina The ability to do something for a long time before tiring

standards Levels of quality

strong-willed Determined

temperament One's personality or nature

terrain The physical features of the land

territorial One who is protective of an area they think is theirs

textile Cloth or fabric

tracking Following something

traits Unique qualities or characteristics

vermin Pests such as rodents and other small animals

watchdog A dog that alerts owners to the presence of something

World War I An international conflict that lasted from 1914 to 1918

World War II An international conflict that lasted from 1939 to 1945

INDEX

African breeds, 52–57, 60–61, 86

American breeds, 18–21, 40–41, 48–49, 100, 106–7, 109, 142–43, 161, 170–71

Arctic breeds, 82–83, 86, 161, 184

art, dogs in, 114, 132–33, 146–47

Asian breeds, 62–63, 84–86, 114, 118–19, 122–23, 137, 148–49, 154–55, 158–59, 160

Australian breeds, 174–75

Belgian breeds, 136, 176–77

blood sport, dogs in, 70–71, 108, 110–13, 144–45

breed standards, 5, 6, 8, 188

breeders, 188

circus dogs, 126, 146–47, 150–51

Cuban breeds, 128–29

dog sports, 6, 22, 33, 35–36, 56, 72, 76, 89, 90, 112, 117, 127, 129, 135, 151, 153, 165–66, 172, 175, 183

English breeds, 21, 24–25, 30–31, 40–41, 52, 100–3, 109, 112–13, 116–17, 126–27, 134–35, 144–45, 166–67, 172–73, 180–81

French breeds, 44–45, 86, 132–33, 140–41, 151, 178–79, 184

German breeds, 33–35, 50–51, 66–69, 72–75, 87, 136, 150–51, 161, 164–65

guard dogs, 8, 56–57, 64, 66–73, 86, 164–65

guide dogs, 9, 14–17, 164–65, 170–71

Hungarian breeds, 36–37, 87, 182–83, 185

Irish breeds, 27–29, 58–59, 73, 101, 104–5

kennel clubs, 6, 31, 106, 135, 140, 173, 188

mascots, dogs as, 50–51, 110–11, 142–45, 152–53

Mexican breeds, 120–21, 156–57

military dogs, 14–15, 164–65, 176–77

mixed breeds, 4, 186–87, 189

police dogs, 8–9, 68–69, 102–3, 164–65, 176–77

prey drive, 6, 35, 38, 42, 53–54, 107

rescue organizations, 188

rodeo dogs, 170–71

Scottish breeds, 26, 53, 94–97, 168–69, 172–73, 185

search-and-rescue dogs, 8, 14–17, 46–47, 80–81, 164–65, 170–71

service dogs, 8, 14–15, 74–75, 106–7, 164–65

shelters, 188–89

spitz-type dogs, 124–25, 160

Swiss breeds, 78–81, 87

therapy dogs, 8, 14–17, 30–31, 42–43, 68–71, 80–81, 112–13, 116–17, 128–29, 132–33, 148–49, 168–71

TV and movies, dogs in, 17, 25, 47, 73, 93, 98–99, 150, 165, 169

US presidents, dogs of, 29

war, dogs in, 58–59, 66–69, 74–77, 102–3, 178–79

watchdogs, 26, 36–37, 87, 94–95, 104–5, 130–31, 139, 148–49, 152–53, 158–59, 166–67, 178–79